# THE NEXT WORLD WAR

THE NEXT WORLD WAR
PUBLISHED BY WATERBROOK PRESS
12265 Oracle Boulevard, Suite 200
Colorado Springs, Colorado 80921
*A division of Random House Inc.*

All Scripture quotations are taken from the King James Version. Verses quoted from the Koran are taken from the translation by George Sale, available at www.gutenberg.org/etext/7440.

10-Digit ISBN: 1-4000-7106-2
13-Digit ISBN: 978-1-4000-7106-7

Library of Congress Cataloging-in-Publication Data
Jeffrey, Grant R.
   The next world war : what prophecy reveals about extreme Islam and the West / Grant R. Jeffrey. — 1st ed.
      p. cm.
   Includes bibliographical references.
   ISBN 1-4000-7106-2
   1. Armageddon. 2. End of the world. 3. Bible—Prophecies. 4. Islamic fundamentalism.
5. Civilization, Western—Forecasting. I. Title.
   BS649.A68J44 2006
   236'.9—dc22

                                        2006019196

Printed in the United States of America
2006—First Edition

10 9 8 7 6 5 4 3 2 1

*I dedicate this book to my late, beloved father, Lyle E. Jeffrey, who went to his reward in heaven two years ago. From the time I was eight years of age, my father discussed prophecy with me, and we spent many hours discussing world events in light of ancient prophecies. My father inspired a lifelong fascination with the truths of the Bible's teaching about the events that will occur during the final years leading to the return of the Messiah and the setting up of His kingdom on earth.*

*This book explores the Bible's prophecies relating to the greatest challenge in many centuries, a challenge that now confronts Western civilization. Extremist Islamists are determined to destroy our civilization and our political and religious freedoms. The Bible's prophecies have much to tell us about this challenge and what the future holds.*

# Contents

PART III: THE DEEPER SIGNIFICANCE OF GLOBAL TERROR
*Extreme Islam's Declaration of War Is Foretold in Prophecy*

PART IV: OUR GENERATION HAS ENTERED THE LAST DAYS
*Clear Signs of the Fulfillment of Biblical Prophecy*

# Introduction

# THE NEXT WORLD WAR

The threat of world war is nothing new. In the last century, more than eighty-three million people were slaughtered in two world wars.[1] The duration and reach of these wars—not to mention their unprecedented levels of violence and destruction—were so great that they impacted the lives of billions of people in more than one hundred nations.

Armed conflict continued to break out after World War II, of course. But compared to the devastation of the two world wars, we have enjoyed six decades of relative peace. That is, until now. The events of September 11, 2001, and the ongoing insurgencies in Iraq and Afghanistan represent just two of the more dramatic fronts of the new world war—the one that is unfolding all around us.

A dedicated group of more than one hundred thousand Islamic terrorists has declared all-out war against the West, specifically against Christians and Jews. It is no exaggeration to call the ongoing conflict between extremist Islam and the West the next world war, because it involves almost every nation on earth. Terrorists are committed to using every method of attack at their disposal: suicide bombings, assassinations, and a variety of military operations, as well as computer attacks. They will attempt to disrupt computer systems that control vital communications linking Western banks, stock exchanges, and governments. We are vulnerable to computer viruses, including worms and logic bombs that can cripple essential systems for days, causing massive economic losses. And, of course, there is the chilling prospect that terrorists are on the verge of utilizing weapons of mass destruction (WMD).

The strategic goal of Islamic terrorists is nothing less than the annihilation of Judeo-Christian Western civilization. Although a great deal of the escalating conflict fails to attract media attention and thus occurs "in the shadows," virtually every nation on earth has marshaled its military, police forces, and intelligence agencies to counter this unprecedented threat.

Everything we value—our freedoms and our way of life—is under attack by Muslim extremists. Led by Osama bin Laden's al Qaeda network, these terrorists have dedicated themselves to the destruction of Christians, Jews (especially those in the State of Israel), and all other non-Muslims. The extremists make up a tiny percentage of the 1.2 billion Muslims worldwide. The vast majority are not at war with the West, and they reject al Qaeda's terrorist ideology and tactics. However, as a result of relentless, extremist Islamic teaching in mosques worldwide during the last two decades,[2] millions of young Islamic men in both the East and the West have embraced an ideology that calls for war to the death against all non-Muslims.

But it doesn't stop there. Even moderate Muslims find themselves in al Qaeda's cross hairs simply for refusing to support the global jihad. In the eyes of extremist Islam, refusing to join the jihad is evidence of a person's apostasy from the original teachings of Muhammad.

In the chapters that follow, we will explore who the terrorists are and why they hate the Western way of life. We will look at their motives, goals, and strategies. We will explore the evidence that al Qaeda plans to defeat Christianity and replace it with a global Islamic dictatorship. As we look at current developments, we also will examine the history of Islamic jihad against the West and the biblical prophecies that warn of an overwhelming Islamic invasion of Israel. This full-scale military invasion will involve forces from Arab and North African nations, Iran, and Russia.

The popular Western view of Islam is that, given enough time, even the most radical elements will decide to coexist peacefully with their enemies. We hear this view set forth in the news media and in countless political speeches. History tells the story of fourteen hundred years of violent encounters between Muslims and their non-Muslim (and even some Muslim) neighbors. But despite the testimony of history and the Koran's fundamental teaching of "holy war," or jihad, many Western commentators prefer to imagine that if we insist on seeing Islam as a peaceful religion, it will tend to behave as one.

History shows that from the time Islam was first taught by Muhammad the prophet, it was believed that the new faith was destined to conquer and supplant all other religions. The prophet proclaimed his new faith of conquest and submission to Allah with the Koran in one hand and a sword in the other. Jihad has as its primary goal the Islamic domination of the entire world.

Given the central importance of jihad to Islam, the Western view that it is somehow possible to assimilate extreme Islam into the worldwide democratic system is completely unrealistic. The current manifestations of holy war are not an aberration of modern Islam that arose over the last few decades. Rather, jihad represents the core goal of fundamentalist Islam through the past fourteen centuries. Jihad is how Muhammad and his successors gained control of portions of Spain, northern Africa, and the Middle East during the first hundred years of Islam's existence. While it's true that many Islamic communities downplayed or ignored the goal of jihad when they were militarily weak, the holy-war mandate remains a core doctrine of Islam. All that is needed to fuel jihad are the right circumstances and the rise of motivated leaders. The Islamic revolution in Iran in 1979 gave rise to Ayatollah Ruhollah Khomeini, and Osama bin Laden rose to leadership in the 1980s.

Muslim scholar Bassam Tibi has written: "Muslims are religiously obliged to disseminate the Islamic faith throughout the world.... If non-Muslims submit to conversion or subjugation, this call can be pursued peacefully. If they do not, Muslims are obliged to wage war against them."[3] The unfortunate truth is that global peace, according to Islamic teaching, can be "reached only with the conversion or submission of all mankind to Islam."[4]

Citizens of the West and all other people who cherish religious freedom, political freedom, and basic liberties need to realize that extremists have already launched a world war to achieve a global totalitarian Islamic government. They are dedicated to our destruction.

Strangely, in the language of Islam, Muslims do not consider their violent attacks on Israel and the West as aggressive war (*harb* in Arabic) but choose to regard such attacks as simply Muslims defending their faith. Muslims use the term *harb* to describe any military action taken by non-Muslims against Muslims. In contrast, Islam regards military or terrorist attacks against non-Muslims merely as acts of "opening" the rest of the world to Islam. Those who resist Islamic forces are considered the moral cause of war, and, as such, they must bear the responsibility for the violent struggle. This is the equivalent of a mugger assigning guilt to his victim for daring to use physical force to defend his life and property.

All non-Muslims and all non-Islamic nations, merely by existing, are considered to be at war against Islam. Muslims refer to the non-Muslim world as the dar ul-harb, the "world of war." When Muslims wage jihad, they believe they are bringing about the peace of global Islam. By that definition, whatever Muslims do is an act of peace, and whatever non-Muslims do is an act of war. This helps explain why even moderate Muslims in the West seldom admit that Muslim terrorists are actually terrorists. This dichotomized view of violence makes it almost impossible for Muslims to engage in fair peace negotiations with non-Muslims. Anyone who closely studies Palestinian and Israeli peace negotiations will recognize this problem.

History demonstrates that even a centuries-long era of Muslim military weakness did not destroy the deep-seated desire for violent jihad. Muslim scholar C. Snouck Hurgronje wrote during World War I, "Even if they admit the improbability [of world conquest] at present, they are comforted and encouraged by the recollection of the lengthy period of humiliation that the Prophet himself had to suffer before Allah bestowed victory upon his arms."[5]

The West and its allies, including many moderate Muslim governments, have the military, intelligence, and financial resources to defeat this deadly threat. In the chapters that follow, we will look at the many biblical prophecies that reveal why and how the West will win the next world war.

As serious as the threat is, God is far stronger than our enemies. Prophecy from both the Old and New Testaments reveals that extreme Islam is playing a significant role in the unfolding of events that God foretold more than two thousand years ago. Every newspaper headline that tells of yet another act of terrorism is an indirect reference to the buildup of violence that will lead to a decisive military showdown between Israel and her enemies.

There is a growing fascination with biblical prophecies regarding the events that will transpire in the last days. As we read prophecy, we realize that the things that are happening today and the things that are about to happen have eternal meaning. The primary reason I present my research is to help people recognize Jesus Christ's imminent return. So I encourage you to give this book to friends and family who have not yet placed their faith in Jesus Christ.

I also hope this book will serve as a useful tool to help you witness effectively to others. The growing political-military crisis in the Middle East raises important questions in the minds of people who don't know God. I trust this book will increase your confidence to share your faith with others during the challenging days that lie ahead. Jesus Christ is the only true security in an uncertain world.

# PART I

---

# THE ANCIENT BEGINNING
# OF THE LAST DAYS

*Genesis and the Future*

Many historians point to 1948 and the founding of the modern State of Israel as the development that triggered the current escalation of violence in the Middle East. But students of prophecy know that the enmity between Jews and Arabs predates by millenniums even the birth of Islam. Both Jews and Arabs are descendants of Abraham, and God prophesied in Genesis that Ishmael and Isaac and their descendants would live in conflict.

In the first section of this book, we will look at the ancient origins of enmity between Ishmael and Isaac and, by extension, between the nations that today represent their descendants. We also will look at the birth of the modern Jewish state, the 1948 flash point that gave new impetus to violent clashes in the Middle East. And finally, at the end of part 1, we will look at amazing prophecies contained in the Muslim scriptures, which foretell an astounding victory of Israel over its Muslim enemies.

# The Roots of Arab Muslim Hatred

*Enmity Between Ishmael and Isaac Has Come Home to Roost*

The most dangerous threat facing the modern world has its origins in a four-thousand-year-old conflict between two half brothers. The ancient blood feud between Ishmael and Isaac is now being played out on the world stage. God told His people thousands of years ago that there would be an implacable hatred between the sons of Abraham. Ishmael, the son of the Egyptian Hagar, would burn with enmity toward his brother, Isaac, the son of Sarah and the ancestor of the Jewish people.

Millenniums of hatred are now culminating in the violent dispute involving the Palestinians and their Arab brethren against their Jewish neighbors. As we look closely at the origins of this war, we will gain greater understanding of how God has set the stage for the final resolution of this struggle in the events of the last days.

## Two Brothers—The Root of Enmity

The patriarch Abraham is the father of the two great Semitic peoples who have contested the land of Israel and the surrounding territory for much of recorded history. God promised Abraham that He would give him so many descendants they could not possibly be numbered. God declared, "And I will make thy seed as the dust of the earth: so that if a man can number the dust of the earth, then shall thy seed also be numbered" (Genesis 13:16). However, Abraham and his wife, Sarah, were far beyond the normal age of childbearing. Sarah laughed when the Lord promised her a son because her ability to reproduce had long since ceased.

When the fulfillment of God's promise seemed to be delayed, Abraham and Sarah decided to use Sarah's Egyptian handmaiden, Hagar, in an ancient custom. Abraham had sexual relations with Hagar in order to father a son who could make God's promise possible. Hagar gave birth to Ishmael, and when Ishmael had grown into a young man, God fulfilled His earlier prophecy, and Sarah gave birth to the promised "seed," Isaac. Sarah resented Ishmael as a potential threat to Isaac's standing as Abraham's heir, so a bitter rivalry arose between Sarah and Hagar. Sarah convinced Abraham to exile Hagar and Ishmael from their settlement. However, God provided for the needs of Hagar and her son and declared that He would raise up twelve great nations from Ishmael's descendants.

The Lord also prophesied that Ishmael would be a violent man who would be in constant conflict with his brethren (see Genesis 16:12). The history of the last forty centuries has borne out this prophecy. Whenever Israel was defeated by her many enemies, her Arab neighbors would join in the attack and take advantage of her weakness. In tragic fulfillment of King David's prophecy in Psalm 83, the Arab nations surrounding Israel have joined in a bitter confederacy with the intention of removing Israel from the region.

In the Middle East, tradition requires that revenge for some ancient crime by an enemy tribe must be pursued by the descendants of the aggrieved tribe even if decades or centuries have passed. The Arabs have a saying that illustrates this tradition: "The Arab got his revenge—fifty years later." An Arab friend once discussed this prevailing desire for revenge and quoted a familiar saying: "Revenge is a dish best served cold."[1] Recognizing the intense and lasting demand for revenge helps explain why it is so difficult to negotiate true peace between the Arabs and the Jews.

In Genesis 16, God described Ishmael, the father of the Arabs:

> And the angel of the LORD said unto [Hagar], Behold, thou art with child, and shalt bear a son, and shalt call his name Ishmael; because the LORD hath heard thy affliction. And he will be a wild man; his hand will be against every man, and every man's hand against him; and he shall dwell in the presence of all his brethren. (verses 11–12)

Ishmael would be an enemy to his neighbors, and his neighbors would be at enmity with him. But God also promised to bless Ishmael through his descendants. God would ultimately provide the Arabs with an inheritance in the Promised Land that would be ruled by the seed of Isaac under the Messiah, Jesus Christ (see Ezekiel 47:22–23).

God also prophesied in Genesis 17 that He would bless Ishmael: "And as for Ishmael, I have heard thee: Behold, I have blessed him, and will make him fruitful, and will multiply him exceedingly; twelve princes shall he beget, and I will make him a great nation" (verse 20).

## IDENTIFYING THE ENEMY NATIONS

The Lord told Hagar that her son "will be a wild man; his hand will be against every man, and every man's hand against him" (Genesis 16:12). Tragically, this prophecy has been fulfilled in the thousands of years of hatred between the Arabs and the Jews. The apostle Paul illustrated this age-old hatred in his letter to the Galatians: "But as then he that was born after the flesh [the Arabs] persecuted him that was born after the Spirit [the Jews], even so it is now" (Galatians 4:29). The Arab peoples lived as nomads; they never set up an independent nation or established a capital in the land of Israel.

It is interesting to note that although Egypt is typically considered an Arab nation, it is not. As Max Dimont observed in his excellent book *Jews, God, and History,* "Strictly speaking, Egypt…is not an Arab nation, though 90 percent of its people follow the Moslem faith and speak Arabic. The vast majority of today's Egyptians are of Hamitic descent [or descendants of Noah's son Ham], with the Arab Bedouins composing the largest minority group. Only a small minority, the Copts, are true descendants of the ancient Egyptians."[2]

In addition to the Arabs descended from the Ishmaelites, the Bible describes other related groups that will rise up in the last days as enemies of Israel. In particular, the Scriptures describe an alliance of Islamic nations that will come against Israel after the Jewish exiles return to the land. Three thousand years ago David prophesied that these nations would form a confederacy against Israel:

> They have said, Come, and let us cut them off from being a
> nation; that the name of Israel may be no more in remem-
> brance. For they have consulted together with one consent: they
> are confederate against thee: the tabernacles of Edom, and the
> Ishmaelites; of Moab, and the Hagarenes; Gebal, and Ammon,
> and Amalek; the Philistines with the inhabitants of Tyre; Assur
> also is joined with them: they have holpen the children of Lot.
> (Psalm 83:4–8)

This ancient list of nations is fascinating, as it enumerates almost all the modern Islamic nations (identified in parentheses below) that oppose Israel's existence:

Edom—from Esau, the brother of Jacob (Jordan)

Ishmaelites—descended from Ishmael, son of Hagar (the Arabs)

Moab—son of Lot (Jordan east of the Dead Sea)

Hagarenes—descended from one of the twelve sons of Hagar

Gebal—ancient Byblus (north of Beirut)

Ammon—son of Lot (capital of Jordan)

Amalek—descended from Esau (southern Jordan)

Philistines—from Ham (throughout Palestine, Syria)

Tyre—a Phoenician city (Lebanon)

Assur—founded Assyria (Iraq and Iran)

Children of Lot—Moab and Ammon (Jordan)

Ezekiel referred to this coming conflict in Ezekiel 38, where he named additional Islamic allies including Iran (ancient Persia), the Islamic nations of North Africa, and the military leadership of Russia. (This fascinating prophecy is examined in detail in chapter 12 of this book.) Ezekiel was given a great vision that included the Arab hatred of Israel, Israel's exile from the Promised Land, and her final miraculous return from the valley of dry bones in the last days before the return of the Messiah. In Ezekiel 35, significantly placed near the prophecy of the restoration of the captives, the Lord describes His coming judgment against the Arab nations (including Edom, or Mount Seir, which is in present-day Jordan) because of their centuries-old hatred of the Jews.

In a prophetic vision, Ezekiel saw the events of the last days. The Jews would return to the Promised Land and would find themselves violently opposed by the surrounding Arab nations, which would demonstrate a "perpetual hatred" that would motivate them to "shed the blood of the children of Israel by the force of the sword in the time of their calamity" (Ezekiel 35:5).

The prophet Ezekiel wrote these words twenty-five centuries ago:

> Moreover the word of the LORD came unto me, saying, Son of
> man, set thy face against mount Seir, and prophesy against it, and
> say unto it, Thus saith the Lord GOD; Behold, O mount Seir, I
> am against thee, and I will stretch out mine hand against thee,
> and I will make thee most desolate. I will lay thy cities waste, and
> thou shalt be desolate, and thou shalt know that I am the LORD.
> Because thou hast had a perpetual hatred, and hast shed the

# THE NEXT WORLD WAR

---

**WHAT PROPHECY REVEALS**
**ABOUT EXTREME ISLAM**
**AND THE WEST**

---

# GRANT R. JEFFREY

BEST-SELLING AUTHOR OF *APOCALYPSE*

WATERBROOK
PRESS

blood of the children of Israel by the force of the sword in the time of their calamity, in the time that their iniquity had an end:...

Because thou hast said, These two nations and these two countries shall be mine, and we will possess it; whereas the LORD was there. (Ezekiel 35:1–5, 10)

The "two countries" refers to Israel and Judah, the two parts of the divided kingdom of Israel after the reign of King Solomon. Although Jordan is at present an ally of the West in the war against terrorism, its underlying anti-Semitism has motivated Jordan in the past to join in repeated wars against Israel, and the same thing will happen again. Ezekiel prophesied that Jordan will join the confederacy against Israel.

## THE ARAB-ISLAMIC CONSPIRACY TO DESTROY ISRAEL

Satan hates Israel because the Jews are the seed of promise and have been the recipients and preservers of the sacred Word of God for all humanity. From the beginning, Satan has stirred Ishmael's descendants to bitterly hate and to kill the Jews.

The Word of God prophesies that in the final days, the seed of Ishmael will join with a number of allies, including Russia, in an attempt to destroy the people of God before the Messiah returns. Despite the size of their armies and the advantages of Russian military technology, the soldiers of Gog and Magog will be destroyed (see Ezekiel 38–39). King David prophesied that God will supernaturally intervene to save Israel. God has promised to destroy all those who seek to conquer "the houses of God" in the land of the Jews (see Psalm 83:12).

The genocidal hatred that seeks the total destruction of the Jews stands alone in the history of national conflicts. Throughout history, when a nation or group lost a battle or a war, they surrendered cities, territory, treasure, and legal rights. However, the Arab and Palestinian leadership have repeatedly declared they will annihilate every Jewish man, woman, and child if they ever defeat Israel in battle. The history of Arab massacres of Israeli soldiers and civilians who have surrendered to them confirms that their threats of genocide are not verbal exaggerations but rather their policy and practice.

Ezekiel received a prophecy regarding the future conflict during the last days when the Arabs will join a tremendous, multinational, Islamic invasion force led by Russia (or ancient Magog; see Ezekiel 38:1–4) and composed primarily of Arabs and soldiers from other Islamic nations.

> Persia, Ethiopia, and Libya with them; all of them with shield
> and helmet: Gomer, and all his bands; the house of Togarmah
> of the north quarters, and all his bands: and many people with
> thee. (Ezekiel 38:5–6)

In chapter 12 of this book we will examine in detail Ezekiel's prophecy of God's supernatural destruction of the invading armies by fire, plague, earthquake, and madness. For now, however, take note of the following passage, which describes the international response to these remarkable supernatural interventions:

> Thus will I magnify myself, and sanctify myself; and I will be
> known in the eyes of many nations, and they shall know that
> I am the LORD. (Ezekiel 38:23)

God's supernatural deliverance of Israel will cause all people throughout the earth to recognize His supremacy (see also Psalm 83:18).

## GOD'S PROMISE OF PROTECTION

God has made it clear that He will preserve His chosen people. Despite all the warnings and prophecies about judgment for Israel's disobedience, God has said repeatedly that He will prosper and protect His people. His un-shakeable promise is "I will give peace in the land."

> Ye shall keep my sabbaths, and reverence my sanctuary: I am the LORD.
>
> If ye walk in my statutes, and keep my commandments, and do them; then I will give you rain in due season, and the land shall yield her increase, and the trees of the field shall yield their fruit. And your threshing shall reach unto the vintage, and the vintage shall reach unto the sowing time: and ye shall eat your bread to the full, and dwell in your land safely. And I will give peace in the land, and ye shall lie down, and none shall make you afraid: and I will rid evil beasts out of the land, neither shall the sword go through your land. (Leviticus 26:2–6)

The Lord promises to bless His people with rain, fertility, and prosperity. He assures them that finally they will enjoy peace and prosperity forever.

### God's Eternal Covenant with the Jews

Despite the centuries of spiritual rebellion and unbelief by the majority of the Jewish people, God has solemnly promised that His covenant with Israel is as unbreakable as His covenant to continue providing day and night and the seasons.

> And the word of the LORD came unto Jeremiah, saying, Thus saith the LORD; If ye can break my covenant of the day, and my covenant of the night, and that there should not be day and night in their season; then may also my covenant be broken with David my servant, that he should not have a son to reign upon his throne; and with the Levites the priests, my ministers. (Jeremiah 33:19–21)

*God Promises Reconciliation*

When Jesus finally establishes His kingdom, He will remove the enmity from the hearts of both Arabs and Jews. Then He will reconcile the sons of Abraham, and they will live at peace in the Holy Land.

> And it shall come to pass, that ye shall divide it by lot for an inheritance unto you, and to the strangers that sojourn among you, which shall beget children among you: and they shall be unto you as born in the country among the children of Israel; they shall have inheritance with you among the tribes of Israel. And it shall come to pass, that in what tribe the stranger sojourn- eth, there shall ye give him his inheritance, saith the Lord GOD. (Ezekiel 47:22–23)

Ezekiel reveals that the Promised Land (from the Mediterranean Sea to the Euphrates River) will be allocated in east-west strips to each of the twelve tribes of the restored Israel. However, the Arabs (the "strangers") will also receive their inheritance of land within Israel.

Finally, with the hatred and desire for revenge supernaturally elimi- nated from the hearts of both Arabs and Jews, the Middle East and the entire world will know true, lasting peace after the victory of Jesus Christ at Armageddon. Then Christ will establish His eternal kingdom as He rules the earth from the throne of David in Jerusalem.

## CURRENT ENMITY BETWEEN MUSLIMS AND JEWS

Until the prophecies come to pass, the bitter hatred that burned in the hearts of Hagar and her son, Ishmael, because of their forced exile from the tent of Abraham and Sarah, still burns in the hearts of most Muslim Arabs. The ancient hatred of Jews was at a low ebb when Muhammad launched his new religion in 622. However, when the Jews around Mecca refused to abandon their faith and submit to Islam, Muhammad declared that the Jews were the enemies of Allah and initiated warfare to force them to submit to Islam or die.

Since that moment, the sons of Ishmael have remained committed to achieving victory over the Jews whenever they encounter them. Since 1948 and the rebirth of Israel, the ancient hatred has been aroused. However, the Arab nations surrounding Israel—and the Palestinians who live within the Jewish state or in the West Bank and Gaza—know they cannot overcome Israel militarily. In addition to superiority in military technology, Israel has the advantage with its powerful army, air force, and navy. Further, Israel possesses at least three hundred nuclear warheads as well as a number of highly secret electronic weapons.[3]

Israel's enemies realize that only a full Islamic confederation, together with the advanced military technology of the Russian army and its millions of well-trained troops, would enable the Arab nations to obtain their dream: the conquest of Jerusalem and the elimination of the Jews from the Middle East. In chapter 12 of this book we will examine plans and preparations for the coming Russo-Islamic invasion of Israel.

## DOES ISRAEL HAVE A LEGITIMATE CLAIM TO THE LAND?

When the modern State of Israel was founded, the surrounding Arab nations argued that the Jews had no legitimate claim to the land. But the Koran states otherwise. Although Islam's holy book and various Muslim commentaries contain numerous condemnations of the Jews and their faith, it is fascinating to note a number of significant passages (suras) in the Koran where Muhammad declares that God granted the Jewish people full possession of the land of Israel.

> Call to mind when Moses said unto his people, O my people,
> remember the favor of GOD towards you, since he hath
> appointed prophets among you, and constituted you kings, and

bestowed on you what he hath given to no other nation in the world.

O my people, enter the holy land, which GOD hath decreed you, and turn not your backs, lest ye be subverted and perish. (Sura 5:20–21)

This passage declares that the land known as Palestine was given to Israel by God and not to any other people. Specifically, the Koran affirms to Israel that God "constituted you kings, and bestowed on you what he hath given to no other nation in the world." This remarkable statement is reinforced and confirmed in several other Koranic passages, including Sura 7:137–38 and Sura 17:104:

And we caused the people who had been rendered weak to inherit the eastern parts of the earth and the western parts thereof, which we blessed with fertility; and the gracious word of thy LORD was fulfilled on the children of Israel, for that they had endured with patience: and we destroyed the structures which Pharaoh and his people had made, and that which they had erected.

And we caused the children of Israel to pass through the sea, and they came unto a people who gave themselves up to the worship of their idols, and they said, O Moses, make us a god, in like manner as these people have gods. (Sura 7:137–38)

And we said unto the children of Israel, after his destruction, Dwell ye in the land: and when the promise of the next life shall come to be fulfilled. (Sura 17:104)

The Koran clearly declares that Allah chose and blessed the Jewish people "and bestowed on you what he hath given to no other nation in the world" (Sura 5:20). In another extraordinary statement, in Sura 45:16, we find these words: "We gave unto the children of Israel the book of the law, and wisdom, and prophecy; and we fed them with good things, and preferred them above all nations."

In the next chapter we will explore the very divisive issue of who truly has the legitimate right to the sovereign control of ancient Palestine. We will examine this critical issue from the standpoint of history, law, and the unchangeable covenant of God as recorded in the Word of God that established a title deed to the land that is eternal.

# GOD BRINGS HIS PEOPLE
# BACK TO THE HOLY LAND

*Who Has the Legitimate Claim to Palestine?*

Four thousand years ago God promised a vast amount of land to Abraham and his descendants. "Lift up now thine eyes, and look from the place where thou art northward, and southward, and eastward, and westward: for all the land which thou seest, to thee will I give it, and to thy seed for ever" (Genesis 13:14–15). In making this promise, God was not giving land only to the descendants of Isaac. He was promising land also to the descendants of Ishmael. Indeed, the Arabs became a nomadic people who roamed throughout Palestine and the surrounding region, which encompasses an area five hundred times that of modern-day Israel. Today Arabs inhabit twenty-one countries in the Middle East, with fifty times the population of Israel.

In Genesis 13:15, the Lord promised the land to Abraham and his seed forever. God later renewed the promise, this time giving the land of Israel to the descendants of Isaac, the seed of promise. God said to Isaac, "Sojourn in this land, and I will be with thee, and will bless thee; for unto thee, and unto thy seed, I will give all these countries, and I will perform the oath which I sware unto Abraham thy father" (Genesis 26:3).

The promise was renewed to Isaac's son Jacob, whom God renamed Israel, which means "Prince with God." "And, behold, the LORD stood above it, and said, I am the LORD God of Abraham thy father, and the God of Isaac: the land whereon thou liest, to thee will I give it, and to thy seed" (Genesis 28:13).

Although throughout history the Jews have been repeatedly forced into exile, the prophet Ezekiel makes clear that the Lord promised to restore the Jews to their land:

> And I will bring them out from the people, and gather them
> from the countries, and will bring them to their own land, and
> feed them upon the mountains of Israel by the rivers, and in all
> the inhabited places of the country. (34:13)

## JESUS PROPHESIED THE REBIRTH OF ISRAEL

Jesus Christ, speaking with His Jewish disciples on the Mount of Olives, warned that the Romans would destroy Jerusalem: "There shall not be left here one stone upon another" (Matthew 24:2). However, Christ also prophesied that the fig tree (exclusively a biblical symbol of Israel) would revive in the last days and would be restored again to the Promised Land (see Matthew 24:32–33). Many biblical scholars have interpreted Christ's prophecy as a promise that the Jews would rebuild their ancient homeland in the same generation that would live to witness the return of the Son of Man and the establishment of the promised kingdom of God.

It is interesting to note that an early church teaching about the rebirth of Israel is documented in a manuscript titled the *Apocalypse of Peter*, a commentary written in AD 110 on the Matthew 24 prophecy of the fig tree.

1. And when he was seated on the Mount of Olives, his own came unto him, and we entreated and implored him severally and besought him, saying unto him, "Make known

unto us what are the signs of thy Parousia and of the end of the world, that we may perceive and mark the time of thy Parousia and instruct those who come after us, to whom we preach the word of thy Gospel and whom we install in thy Church, in order that they, when they hear it, may take heed to themselves that they mark the time of thy coming....

2. And ye, receive ye the Parable of the fig-tree thereon: as soon as its shoots have gone forth and its boughs have sprouted, the end of the world will come." And I, Peter, answered and said unto him, "Explain to me concerning the fig-tree, [and] how we shall perceive it, for throughout all its days does the fig-tree sprout and every year it brings forth its fruit for its master. What (then) meaneth the parable of the fig-tree? We know it not." And the Master answered and said unto me, "Dost thou not understand that the fig-tree is the house of Israel?... Hast thou not grasped that the fig-tree is the house of Israel?"[1]

This Christian commentary on Christ's prophecy reveals that in AD 110 (only forty years after the Romans destroyed Jerusalem), while the Jewish capital and the Temple were in ruins, the early church understood that God would restore Israel as a nation just prior to Christ's return.

Ezekiel prophesied that the ultimate redemption of Israel and the return to Palestine from worldwide exile, the Diaspora, would not depend on Israel's obedience or changed heart but rather would occur because God had decided to sanctify His holy name among Israel and the nations. "Therefore say unto the house of Israel, Thus saith the Lord GOD; I do not this for your sakes, O house of Israel, but for mine holy name's sake, which ye have profaned among the heathen, whither ye went" (Ezekiel 36:22).

The great Jewish leader David Ben-Gurion, who became the first prime minister of Israel, testified before the Palestine Royal Commission about

Israel's absolute right to the land: "The Bible is our mandate. The mandate of the League [of Nations] is only a recognition of this right and does not establish new things."[2]

## ISRAEL RETURNS TO THE LAND

Support for the existence of a Jewish state, as well as ongoing support for the nation of Israel, is known as Zionism. In 1896 Theodor Herzl, founder of the movement to revive the Jewish state, wrote a pro-Israel pamphlet, *The Jewish State,* which caused a furor when it was published. The word *Zionism* was coined to express the ardent desire of exiled Jews to return to their historic homeland, the Zion of the Bible. A tremendous number of Jews from Europe and Russia began immigrating to Palestine after Herzl's Zionist declaration. The first Zionist Congress met in Basel, Switzerland, in 1897 to plan in practical terms the revival of the nation of Israel after almost two thousand years of Jewish exile. The vicious persecution of Jews in Russia and Ukraine during the 1880s had already forced hundreds of thousands of Jews to flee for their lives to Palestine and North America. The Zionist movement in Europe greatly accelerated the immigration and assisted in the establishing of new settlements and kibbutzim (communal farms) in Palestine.

After World War I, Great Britain was granted a thirty-year mandate to rule a region that included present-day Israel, the West Bank and Gaza, and modern Jordan. The area was called Transjordan and contained very few inhabitants. Lord Arthur James Balfour, the head of Great Britain's Foreign Office, received approval from the British cabinet and released the following declaration in favor of a Jewish homeland. The declaration, issued on November 2, 1917, is known as the Balfour Declaration:

His Majesty's Government view with favour the establishment in Palestine of a national home for the Jewish people, and will use their best endeavours to facilitate the achievement of this object, it being clearly understood that nothing shall be done which may prejudice the civil and religious rights of existing non-Jewish communities in Palestine or the rights and political status enjoyed by Jews in any other country.[3]

The declaration was endorsed on July 24, 1922, by the League of Nations (the predecessor of the United Nations), the United States, and for a short time even some Arab states. Under the Balfour Declaration and other treaties after World War I, Arab states—including Transjordan, Syria, Iraq, and Saudi Arabia—received almost five hundred times as much land as was granted to the Jewish national homeland. The leader of Saudi Arabia, Emir Faisal, met several times with the Zionist leader, Dr. Chaim Weizmann, who had negotiated the Balfour Declaration. A statement released by Faisal and Weizmann asserted that "the surest means of working out the consummation of their national aspiration is through the closest possible collaboration of the development of the Arab state and Palestine (the Jewish Homeland)."[4]

As the leading figure among the Arabs, Faisal wrote to another Zionist leader, Felix Frankfurter, in 1919, declaring, "The Arabs, especially the educated among us, look with deepest sympathy on the Zionist movement.... We will wish the Jews a hearty welcome home...our two movements complete one another.... And there is room in Syria [which at that time included Palestine] for us both...neither can be a real success without the other."[5]

## WHO HAS THE LEGITIMATE CLAIM TO PALESTINE?

At the end of World War I, the Allies broke up the Ottoman Empire, which had allied itself with Germany. Eighty percent of the land that was initially granted by the League of Nations and Great Britain to the Jewish national homeland was arbitrarily torn away by Britain and given to the Arabs in 1921. The British had promised Emir Faisal that he would be king of Syria. In the diplomatic shuffle after World War I, the French received the mandate to rule Syria, and France set up a separate Arab leadership. In an attempt to placate Faisal, the British offered him the crown of Iraq. Winston Churchill then offered 80 percent of the British Mandate to Faisal's brother, Abdullah, as emir of the newly created territory called Transjordan.

This illegal annexation of 80 percent of the Promised Land helped create the disaster that still troubles the Middle East. Out of some five million square miles of former (Turkish) Ottoman territory, Arab nations received 99.8 percent of the land. This territory is now twenty-one independent countries with a total population in excess of two hundred million. The Arab nations also received the enormous oil reserves that were discovered in the 1930s. Israel received less than one-fifth of one percent of the land— only eight thousand square miles.

The promise of the Balfour Declaration and Britain's legal commitments to the League of Nations had encouraged Jewish immigration to the Jewish national homeland. However, in 1921, 1929, and 1939, Britain drastically changed the rules in order to prevent Jews from immigrating to Palestine. As Arab opposition to Jewish immigration grew, many British government leaders decided it was better for the British Empire to retain the support of the Arab states than that of the Jewish immigrants. In addition, the British ruling circles harbored a great deal of anti-Semitism.

While British authorities used every possible means to prevent Jews from entering Israel, the doors were thrown wide open to allow unlimited Arab immigration from the surrounding nations. A huge number of Arabs flowed into the areas of Palestine where Jewish immigrants were building farms and businesses. With severe restrictions on the immigration of Jews, Jewish businesses and farms in Palestine were unable to obtain sufficient workers and, therefore, hired a large number of Arabs. It is interesting to note that the Arab population increases between 1921 and 1946 were far higher (90 to 200 percent) in Jewish communities such as Jerusalem, Haifa, and Jaffa than in Arab towns. In predominantly Arab towns, such as Nablus and Bethlehem, the Arab population increase averaged only between 32 and 40 percent.

In 1948 the British Mandate government made a survey of Palestine, which revealed the following breakdown of landownership:

- 71.2 percent of the land was owned by Great Britain.
- 8.6 percent was owned by Jews.
- 3.3 percent was owned by resident Arabs.
- 16.9 percent was owned by nonresident Arabs living in Syria, Jordan, and other countries.[6]

When Israel's 1948 War of Independence concluded, land that had been owned by the British Mandate government was transferred by international law to the new government of Israel. Despite Arab claims to the contrary, the Jews purchased the lands they wanted from the former Arab landowners, often at very high prices. In the period after 1967's Six-Day War, Jewish settlements were built almost entirely on government-owned land on the Green Line that marked the interim boundary between Israel and the West Bank, and on former Jordanian army bases along the Jordan River. In the Six-Day War, Israel gained territory around Jerusalem that had been occupied by Jordan between 1948 and 1967. By design, to enhance their security, Jewish settlements in the West Bank and Gaza were often built on isolated sites far from existing Arab villages. Settlements sometimes used former Jordanian army bases to take advantage of the militarily strategic locations and to prevent terrorists from using those sites.

During the 1948 War of Independence, the Arab governments were convinced they would quickly destroy the Jewish population of the young State of Israel. The Arab media and political leaders from surrounding Arab nations appealed to the Arab residents of Palestine to leave their homes so that invading armies could purge the land of all residents without inadvertently attacking Arabs.[7]

While Arab governments advised Arab settlers to flee during the 1948 war, Jews begged their Arab neighbors to remain in the new nation. The Jewish Haifa Workers' Council issued this appeal: "For years we have lived together in our city, Haifa.… Do not fear. Do not destroy your homes with your own hands,…do not bring upon yourself tragedy by unnecessary evacuation and self-imposed burdens.… But in this city, yours and ours, Haifa, the gates are open for work, for life, and for peace for you and your families."[8]

In a report issued by the Arab-financed Institute for Palestine Studies in Beirut, Lebanon, the writers concluded that the majority of the Arab refugees were not expelled by force in 1948 but fled of their own volition. Fully 68 percent of the refugees fled the country, according to the report, without seeing a single Israeli soldier.[9]

On April 27, 1950, the Arab National Committee of Haifa wrote a memorandum to the Arab governments that stated, "The removal of the Arab inhabitants…was voluntary and was carried out at our request.… The Arab delegation proudly asked for the evacuation of the Arabs and their removal to the neighbouring Arab countries."[10] The motivation for Arabs to leave their homes came from the Arab leadership, not from the Jews.[11]

## THE PALESTINE MYTH

Approximately 430,000 Arabs fled Palestine at the time of the 1948 war.[12] This number is significantly lower than most of the estimates given out after the war. Arab organizations often inflated their refugee estimates for political reasons. And on an individual level, local Bedouins and Arabs living close to United Nations refugee camps often claimed refugee status in order to gain significant financial benefits.

U.N. officials estimated that many of the refugees on the relief rolls were fictitious. For instance, births were always reported, but deaths seldom were. Families would conceal deaths so they could continue receiving food and fuel rations. Some reports claimed that certain Arabs possessed as many as five hundred individual ration cards, entitling them to receive enormous benefits.[13] One factor to consider is that the vast majority of officials overseeing the dispersal of U.N. refugee funds were Palestinians or Arabs of Syrian, Lebanese, Egyptian, or Jordanian background.[14]

After World War II, which resulted in population movements of millions of refugees, national governments and U.N. agencies developed a universal definition of *refugee*. A person who was forced to leave his "permanent or habitual" home was classified as a refugee. However, a significant change of definition took place in the case of the Palestinian Arabs. After the 1948 War of Independence, an Arab refugee was defined as anyone who had left his home or habitation, even if he had lived there for only two years prior to the 1948 conflict. This change in definition was acknowledged by the United Nations Relief and Works Agency in the Special Report of the Director, UNRWA 1954–55, U.N. Document A/2717.

This simple change of definition vastly increased the number of Arabs who could qualify as refugees. The underlying reason for this change is that U.N. officials recognized that a tremendous number of so-called Arab refugees had only recently entered Palestine, in the few years before 1948, before the British Mandate ended. The British wanted to help these people, even though they did not qualify for aid under the conventional definition of refugees.

In 1960 King Hussein of Jordan stated that the Arab nations that had rejected the existence of a Jewish state had added to the plight of Palestinian refugees by keeping them in refugee camps and not allowing them to integrate as Arab citizens in the countries where they had settled. "Since 1948 Arab leaders have approached the Palestine problem in an irresponsible manner...," Hussein stated. "They have used the Palestine people for selfish political purposes. This is ridiculous and, I could say, even criminal."[15]

Arab nations used the displaced Palestinians as pawns in a propaganda war against Israel. Palestinian refugees were victimized by Arab nations and not by the creation of the State of Israel.

―――

The State of Israel has been falsely accused of many things. The Israelis are said to have stolen the land from the rightful Arab owners. They are accused of occupying the Holy Land illegally, of forcing Arab citizens out at the time of the 1948 War of Independence, and of creating circumstances that have made life intolerable for Arab refugees. But a close look at the facts tells a completely different story.

Arab nations bordering Israel have not only manipulated the facts, but they also have used displaced Arabs to gain political leverage against Israel. And, as we will see later in this book, the differences run far deeper than simple political opposition. The Arab leaders are not interested primarily in gaining political advantage; they are devoted to the annihilation of the Jews and the nation of Israel.

In the following chapter we will examine a remarkable series of Islamic prophecies (many obviously derived from the prophecies in Ezekiel, Daniel, Matthew, and the book of Revelation) that refer to a cataclysmic conflict between the forces of Islam and the West, including Israel. This prophetic expectation of key biblical prophetic events may prepare millions of Muslims to accept the revelation of God's supernatural deliverance of Israel in these "last days."

# 3

# KORANIC PROPHECIES
# OF ISLAM'S DEFEAT

*Amazingly, the Muslim Scriptures*
*Predict the Return of Christ*

The Koran speaks of the last days and provides numerous prophetic signs of the approaching apocalypse. To an extent, the prophetic signs in the Koran and the Muslim commentaries parallel and are derived from the prophecies found in the Old and New Testaments of the Bible.

Islam teaches that the day of resurrection is known only to God. Muhammad is said to have asked the angel Gabriel about its timing and was told that no one but God Himself knows the day. But Islam does teach that a series of prophetic events will precede God's judgment and will serve as a warning of the approaching appointment with God.

In light of the crisis in the Middle East and the rise of Muslim fundamentalism from North Africa to Indonesia, it is important that we understand the Islamic beliefs that underlie the profound political, military, and religious movements that are influencing Islam's violent struggle with the West.

## PROPHECIES OF THE APOCALYPSE

Muslim writings speak about the decay of faith and the rise of sensuality in conjunction with the appearance of tumults and seditions around the globe. There will be a great war with the Turks, and great distress will appear everywhere. A prophecy in the hadith commentaries mentions that both Iraq and Syria will be engulfed in insurrection. The predictions include signs in the heavens that parallel the biblical prophecies (namely Luke 21:11).

There will be war with the Europeans (the Greeks), and seventy thousand Jews will capture Constantinople. During the military victory, the hadith commentaries prophesy, the Antichrist will arise. The Antichrist, called al-Masih al-Dajjal (the false or lying Christ), will have only one eye and will be marked on the forehead with the letters CFR, which stands for Cafer, or infidel. He will be the last of a series of antichrists. The Islamic prophecies claim the Jews will initially accept the Antichrist as Messiah ben David, believing he will be the one who will restore the kingdom to Israel. The Antichrist will appear near Iraq and Syria, will ride on a colt, will be followed by seventy thousand Jews, will lay waste many places, and finally will be killed by Jesus Christ, who is to encounter him at a gate (possibly the sealed Eastern Gate of the Temple Mount).

### Islamic Prophecy of Gog and Magog

The Koran and its commentaries describe a terrible war between the Jews and the Islamic armies, together with barbarian armies from Yajuj and Majuj (Gog and Magog). The vast invading armies will drain the Sea of Tiberius (Galilee) for drinking water and will then attack Jerusalem. Jesus Christ and God will together supernaturally destroy the invading Islamic army. After God's victory, the great number of slain bodies of the invading army will provide food for predatory animals and birds. It will take seven years to burn the weapons, and God will cleanse the earth with rain to rid it of the pollution created by the overwhelming slaughter (see Sura 18). Obviously, this prophetic tradition is derived from Ezekiel 38–39.

## Islamic Prophecy of the Return of Christ

The Koran prophesies that Jesus Christ will descend from heaven to earth to usher in His kingdom and judge humanity. It is suggested that Jesus will descend to earth somewhere near Damascus, Syria. He will then defeat the armies of the Antichrist and will kill him. After that victory, Jesus will usher in His kingdom and will provide security, prosperity, and peace. The hatred and malice that have oppressed humanity will finally be destroyed, and nature will be tamed with lions and lambs coexisting in peace (see Sura 39). This prediction parallels the biblical prophecies of Isaiah 65:17 and Revelation 20 concerning the coming millennial kingdom.

Remarkably, the Islamic writings suggest that Arabs will return to their ancient pagan worship. A further passage predicts that the Kaaba of Mecca, which was the focus of ancient worship by pagan Arabs, will be destroyed by the armies of Ethiopia during the crisis of the last days.[1]

## The Coming of the Mahdi

The Mahdi (the Director) is a figure who will appear in the last days, according to Islamic tradition and commentaries, although he is not mentioned directly in the Koran. He is believed to be a direct descendant of Muhammad the prophet (Muhammad Abu'lkasem), and the last of the twelve imams (spiritual leaders), and born in year 255 of Hijra (the Arab calendar). The Mahdi is believed to be the one who is guided by Allah and will rule the coming global Islamic government (the caliphate). The Koran teaches there will be a period of judgment of the Islamic caliphate that will last one thousand years following the great crisis that ends this age (see Sura 32). This reminds us of the New Testament prophecy of the Millennium (Revelation 20).

One of the basic tenets of the Koran is that in the last days there will be a resurrection of all men to participate in a general judgment before God. Muhammad taught that after death, an interview is held in which the departed is examined while sitting up in the grave. The interrogators are two terrible angels named Monker and Nakir. In accordance with this belief, many Muslims used to make sure their graves would be built in such a manner that a corpse would have sufficient room to sit up.

## PARALLELS TO BIBLICAL PROPHECY

Although there are a number of unusual features in Islamic eschatology, many of the prophecies appear to be derived from prophecies in the Old and New Testaments. It is interesting that the hadith commentaries give prominence to Jesus, the Antichrist, the Millennium, and the coming War of Gog and Magog. Since Muhammad quoted extensively from the biblical prophets Ezekiel, Daniel, Joel, Isaiah, and Jesus, it is not surprising that many of the Jewish and Christian apocalyptic features can be found in Islamic writings.

Revelation 7 declares that during the terrible period known as the Great Tribulation, the 144,000 Jewish witnesses from the twelve tribes of Israel will witness to the whole world about the coming kingdom of Christ. The apostle John prophesies that the response to the teaching of these witnesses and to the supernatural proclamation of three angelic messengers will produce the greatest spiritual revival in the history of the world. John declares that the great multitude, too numerous to be numbered and representing all nations, peoples, and tongues, will stand before the throne "and before the Lamb" (Revelation 7:9).

The angel identifies this immense group as "they which came out of great tribulation" (Revelation 7:14). Who will respond to this last-days out-pouring of the message of God? I believe the primary responders will come from the unevangelized peoples of the third world. The angel states that they will come from "all nations, and kindreds, and people, and tongues" (Revelation 7:9). However, it is unlikely that an enormous number of those who already rejected the gentle claims of Christ during the age of grace will suddenly accept faith in Jesus during the Tribulation, when faith in Christ will lead to certain persecution and probable martyrdom. It is more likely that the greatest response to the message of God will come from among the great unreached peoples, including Muslims, Buddhists, and Hindus—populations that currently comprise more than half of humanity.

Considering the hadith commentaries' teachings about Jesus and the Antichrist, it is possible that God will use these writings to prepare the hearts and minds of the Muslim people to accept the truth of the gospel message. The Koran and other Islamic writings contain a remarkable number of references to Jesus Christ. What is fascinating is that the writings of Muhammad discuss Jesus' birth, life, teachings, death, and resurrection in great detail. The Koran includes twenty-eight specific references to the life of Jesus. It also repeats the New Testament prophecies about the return of Jesus to save the Jewish people from the invasion of the army of the Antichrist. These writings could prepare Muslims to finally understand who Jesus is when the full truth of the gospel is made known during the Great Tribulation.

## THE KORAN AND JESUS THE MESSIAH

The following quotes from the Koran reveal the historicity of the life of Jesus as acknowledged by Muhammad.

The Koran acknowledges Jesus as a legitimate prophet of God: "Zacharias, and John, and Jesus, and Elias; all of them were upright men" (Sura 6:85).

Jesus is described as the son of Mary and is said to have delivered the true gospel: "We also caused Jesus the son of Mary to follow the footsteps of the prophets, confirming the law which was sent down before him; and we gave him the gospel, containing direction and light; confirming also the law which was given before it, and a direction and admonition unto those who fear God" (Sura 5:46).

Jesus is declared to be the promised Messiah: "When the angels said; O Mary, verily GOD sendeth thee good tidings, that thou shalt bear the Word proceeding from himself; his name shall be CHRIST JESUS the son of Mary, honourable in this world and in the world to come, and one of those who approach near to the presence of GOD" (Sura 3:45).

While the Koran denies that Jesus is the only begotten Son of God, it does accept that Jesus was born supernaturally to a virgin: "She said, How shall I have a son, seeing a man hath not touched me, and I am no harlot?" (Sura 19:20).

The Koran even refers to the resurrection of Jesus: "And peace be on me the day whereon I was born, and the day whereon I shall die, and the day whereon I shall be raised to life. This was JESUS, the son of Mary; the Word of truth, concerning whom they doubt" (Sura 19:33–34).

## ISLAMIC PROPHECY AND THE TEMPLE MOUNT

The Temple Mount is sacred to Jews as well as Muslims. The area, called the Haram ash-Sharif (which means "noble sanctuary"), is the third-most holy site for Muslims after the holy cities of Mecca and Medina in Saudi Arabia. Mecca and Medina were much more closely associated with the life and history of Muhammad and his disciples than was Jerusalem in the years following 622.

However, Muslims believe Muhammad supernaturally visited the Noble Sanctuary in Jerusalem, and according to tradition, he departed in a spiritual journey to the seventh heaven on his white horse, Burak, from the rock that is under the roof of the Dome of the Rock. The Al-Aqsa Mosque at the southern edge of the Temple Mount is believed by Muslim writers to be referred to in the Koran as the "far place" associated with this journey of Muhammad. There are a number of other Islamic structures on the Temple Mount today. Curiously, although Jerusalem is mentioned more than one thousand times in the Jewish Bible, there is no specific mention of it in the Koran.

### The Dome of the Rock

The most prominent and beautiful building on the Temple Mount is the golden Dome of the Rock, under construction for more than fifty years and completed in 691. Caliph Omar, a successor to Muhammad, conquered Israel in 638 and soon began construction of the dome, which today is one of the oldest continuously used religious buildings in the world. While many people refer to the Dome of the Rock as the Mosque of Omar, this is incorrect, because the dome is a shrine used for prayer. The only major ancient mosque is the Al-Aqsa Mosque, situated several hundred yards to the south, in the building on the edge of the southern wall. A mosque is used for preaching, prayers, and other religious services; a shrine is used only for contemplation and prayers.

Caliph Abdal-Malik finished the Dome of the Rock in 691. From that year until 1856, any infidel or nonbeliever in Islam who dared to enter the mosques or the Dome of the Rock was subject to the death penalty. In past centuries, several Western explorers risked their lives to enter the Noble Sanctuary to provide firsthand research about the Temple Mount. But serious explorations took place only after an 1856 Turkish decree allowed people of all faiths to enter the sacred enclosure under controlled conditions.

Muslim scholars agree with the Jews that the sacred rock on the Temple Mount was the place of the binding of Isaac, when God commanded Abraham to sacrifice his son. They also believe that God used the Foundation Stone of Mount Moriah as the foundation upon which He fashioned the entire world. The Koran accepts the historicity of the Temple in Jerusalem, as well as King David and King Solomon. It also contains a distinct prophecy that in the last days, Jesus the Prophet will come to the Temple Mount through the sealed Eastern Gate.

### The Al-Aqsa Mosque

The Al-Aqsa Mosque is known as "the furthest one" because of its position in comparison to the huge central mosque located in Mecca. The Al-Aqsa Mosque was built in 693, only two years after the completion of the Dome of the Rock. The major entrance is in its northern wall, and there visitors must remove their shoes before going into the central sanctuary, whose roof is supported by enormous, white marble pillars. Some of the pillars measure more than five feet in diameter, and several near the main door still bear the scars of bullets fired during the 1951 Palestinian assassination of King Abdullah of Jordan while he was worshiping there.

The Al-Aqsa Mosque is built on top of the underground structure that dates back to the time of the first Temple in 1000 BC. This structure is called the Aqsa-al-kadeem and descends under the Al-Aqsa Mosque toward the southern Temple Wall and the Hulda Gates, which were used by worshipers, including Jesus and His disciples, as the major public entrance to the Temple. These double and triple gates, though sealed for two thousand years at the southern end, still lead diagonally upward from the Southern Wall, under the Al-Aqsa Mosque, ascending to the surface level of the present Temple Mount. The Jewish Midrash Raba declares that these ancient temple gates were "never destroyed."

## THE TEMPLE MOUNT'S SEALED EASTERN GATE

> Then said the LORD unto me; This gate shall be shut, it shall not
> be opened, and no man shall enter in by it; because the LORD,
> the God of Israel, hath entered in by it, therefore it shall be shut.
> It is for the prince. (Ezekiel 44:2–3)

The beautiful Eastern Gate is of vital importance to Muslims, Christians, and Jews alike. The subterranean foundation ashlar stones of this gate date back to the reign of King Solomon (1000 BC).

When Caliph Omar captured Jerusalem and began to build the Dome of the Rock in 638, the Eastern Gate had already been sealed. From time to time the gate would be opened for special occasions, but then a new regime would seal it again. The Crusader kings of the kingdom of Jerusalem opened the gate around 1183, but in recognition of the ancient prophecy of Ezekiel that the Messiah would enter through this sealed gate, they did not allow it to be used for everyday purposes. Its wooden doors were opened only on special religious feast days to allow royal and religious dignitaries to enter the Temple precincts. After the Crusades ended, Islamic leaders permanently sealed the gate. When Suleiman the Magnificent rebuilt the walls of Jerusalem in 1537, his Turkish workmen rebuilt the top portion of the gate using the much smaller stones visible on the topmost levels.

As I stood on the Temple Mount fifteen years ago and examined the inside walls of the Eastern Gate, my Arab guide, Muhammad, told me Muslims believe that God caused the Eastern Gate to be sealed centuries ago to ensure no one other than the Prophet Jesus could enter it. He claimed that the Muslims know it was prophesied that in the last days, after Armageddon, Jesus will enter through the Eastern Gate and then will judge the world.

Directly west across the Temple Mount from the sealed Eastern Gate is the Arabic dome, built over the foundation stone, the Even Sheteyeh, which my research indicates was the original place the ark of the covenant rested in Solomon's Temple. My Muslim guide pointed to this structure and stated, "This is the place where Jesus will judge the nations at the end of the age." When I asked him to elaborate, he pointed to the huge gateway of pillars joined at the top by a massive lintel stone standing on the northern section of the Western Wall, which is called the Balance of the Day of Judgment, or Al-Mizaan. This gateway of pillars stands just a few feet behind and to the west of the ancient Dome of the Tablets structure.

When I asked my guide to explain why Jesus would judge the nations at that precise spot, he told me, "This was the true site of the Holy of Holies in the ancient Temple of King Solomon." I expressed surprise because virtually all Arabic and Jewish sources have claimed that the Dome of the Rock stands on the site of Solomon's Temple. My guide then told me that he and his father had explored the cisterns deep underneath the Dome of the Tablets in the early 1920s, and they had discovered the ancient drainage tunnels that directed the blood from the large number of sacrificed animals to flow eastward from the altar beneath the surface of the Temple Mount, through the subterranean wall, and into the Kidron Valley.

Muhammad told me that "those who knew" were convinced this was the place of the original Temple. If Muslims in general ever came to believe this, it could open the way for Israel to rebuild her sacred Temple on the original site of Solomon's Temple without violating the Dome of the Rock, which is more than one hundred yards to the south. Neither would it disturb the Al-Aqsa Mosque, which is even farther to the south.

Many have questioned the plausibility of the Temple being reconstructed on the Temple Mount virtually side by side with the Dome of the Rock. But it would not be that unusual in the crowded, complicated architecture of competing religious sites in present-day Israel. The tomb of Abraham in Hebron included worship sites for both Muslims and Jews, because both value the site. Additionally, the Church of the Holy Sepulcher in Jerusalem has been shared for almost seventeen hundred years by somewhat antagonistic Christian groups of Armenians, Ethiopians, Copts, Catholics, and Greek Orthodox priests and their competing religious services. Today the Jews worship at the Western Wall while Muslims worship on the Temple Mount less than one hundred yards away.

In Revelation 11, the prophet John was given a vision of the rebuilt Temple, which would be restored during the future Tribulation period. John was told by the angel, "Rise, and measure the temple of God, and the altar, and them that worship therein. But the court which is without the temple leave out, and measure it not; for it is given unto the Gentiles: and the holy city shall they tread under foot forty and two months" (verses 1–2). Notice that the court, which refers to the Court of the Gentiles, was not to be measured. It is intriguing to note that the Dome of the Rock was built by Omar in the area that used to be occupied by the ancient Court of the Gentiles. Perhaps the reason the angel told John not to measure that particular area is because the Dome of the Rock will still occupy that area during the Tribulation, only a few dozen yards from the wall of the rebuilt Temple.

If you approach the sealed Eastern Gate from the outside Eastern Wall of the Temple Mount, you must walk through a Muslim cemetery. Centuries ago the Arab rulers of Jerusalem chose to build a cemetery in front of the sealed Eastern Gate. The cemetery now extends for a considerable distance north and south along the Eastern Wall. The reason for choosing that particular place as a graveyard is that Muslim Arabs are reluctant to accept the implications of the prophecy that Jesus, the Messiah, will some-day enter the Temple Mount through the sealed Eastern Gate to set up His eternal kingdom from His throne in Jerusalem. Because Muslim imams will not defile themselves by passing through a graveyard, the Arab rulers of Jerusalem believed that the graveyard and the sealed gate would prevent the coming of Jesus the Messiah to save His people. An additional moti-vation was the desire of Muslims to be buried as close as possible to the prophesied place of judgment at the resurrection.

When my wife, Kaye, and I approached the sealed Eastern Gate to examine the stones, we noted that an anonymous Israeli had written on the stones in Hebrew: "Welcome, Messiah."

## PROPHECY THAT THE EASTERN GATE WILL BE OPENED

Afterward he brought me to the gate, even the gate that looketh toward the east.... And the glory of the LORD came into the house by the way of the gate whose prospect is toward the east. So the spirit took me up, and brought me into the inner court; and, behold, the glory of the LORD filled the house. (Ezekiel 43:1, 4–5)

Since the Arabs defeated the Crusaders in 1291, the Eastern Gate has been closed. After six centuries, however, Islamic authorities in control of Jeru-salem attempted to violate Ezekiel's prophecy by forcing open the sealed gate. The first attempt occurred on December 9, 1917, when Muslim authorities sought to open the gate to allow access from the east. But the British army captured Jerusalem on the same day and prevented the open-ing of the gate. When the British left Israel in 1948, Jordan took posses-sion of East Jerusalem and the West Bank. Almost twenty years later, during the first few days of the Six-Day War in June 1967, the Jordanian leadership in control of Jerusalem tried and failed to open the sealed gate.

Both times when Arab workmen were preparing to demolish the

*The sealed Eastern Gate can be seen in the center of this photo of the Temple Mount in Jerusalem.*

ancient stones of the sealed gate, the hand of God was revealed. The first attempt, in 1917, was prevented when Jerusalem passed out of Muslim control and into British hands, and in 1967 the second attempt was thwarted when the Israelis captured Jerusalem. The Eastern Gate has remained sealed according to the ancient biblical prophecy.

The Lord declared to the prophet Habakkuk centuries earlier that despite the apparent delay, God's prophecies will ultimately be fulfilled in His time.

> The LORD answered me, and said, Write the vision, and make it plain upon tables, that he may run that readeth it. For the vision is yet for an appointed time, but at the end it shall speak, and not lie: though it tarry, wait for it; because it will surely come, it will not tarry. (Habakkuk 2:2–3)

The Eastern Gate will remain shut until the day appointed by God, when Jesus Christ will return to usher in His long-promised millennial kingdom. At the Second Coming of Christ, the prophecy of Ezekiel will be fulfilled. Jesus Christ will destroy the armies of the Antichrist at the battle of Armageddon. He will then descend on the Mount of Olives and cross the Kidron Valley. And He will enter the Temple Mount through the Eastern Gate.

—*mm*—

In a later chapter we will examine the historical background and prophetic future of the ongoing conflict between Israel and the Arab-Islamic nations. The return of the Jews to the Holy Land and the reestablishment of the nation of Israel in 1948 set the stage for the fulfillment of the prophecies of the last days. Events that are unfolding today will usher in the final conflict between the Arabs and the Jews. A showdown between a Russo-Islamic confederacy and Israel will shake the world to its foundations. This is the coming War of Gog and Magog, which will change our world forever.

This cataclysmic event will help set the stage for the rise of a ten-nation superstate in Europe, taking the form of a revived Roman Empire, which will be ruled by the coming Antichrist. His conquest of the world for seven years and his final defeat by the return of Jesus at the battle of Armageddon will usher in the long-awaited kingdom of God on earth.

In the following chapter we will explore the deep historical roots of the current extremist Islamic terrorism that has transformed our Western world in the last two and a half decades. September 11, 2001, was a devastating wake-up call to our Western civilization. If we are to come to a full understanding of the "clash of civilizations" that is the major challenge of our generation, we need to explore the fundamental teachings of Islam that motivate those who are now attacking Western society.

# PART II

# THE ORIGINS OF ISLAMIC TERRORISM

*Why It's Necessary to Understand Islam
Before Studying Terrorism*

No one questions that the conflict between Jews and Arabs has ancient origins. But what many observers overlook is that violent conquest—fueled by a hatred of all perceived enemies of Islam—makes brutal terrorist opposition to Jews and Israel a legitimate course of action in the minds of millions of militant Muslims.

In its earliest days, Islam extended its reach through war. And today, the segments of Islam that strategize and carry out terrorist attacks against Israel and the West find warrant for their actions in the Koran and in the history of Islam. Far more than simply a political war or a battle over territory or a conflict fueled by ethnic differences, this is a religious-political war that takes the form of conquest through terrorism and the overthrow of moderate Islamic governments by elections and subversion.

# THE WARRIOR PROPHET

*Muhammad and His Strategy of Conversion by Conquest*

The Islamic struggle to overcome non-Muslim cultures is not a recent development. Ever since the seventh century, when Muhammad proclaimed the Koran to be God's ultimate revelation, followers of Islam have joined a global struggle to defeat Christianity, Judaism, and all other religions—including Hinduism, Buddhism, paganism, and atheism. The struggle currently involves hundreds of millions of Muslims throughout the world who are sympathetic to the cause. Of these, more than one hundred thousand have received terrorist training. Bernard Lewis, an Islamic scholar at Princeton University, notes that the struggle commenced "with the advent of Islam, in the seventh century, and has continued virtually to the present day."[1]

During the first few years of the new Muslim religion, Muhammad relied on teaching and persuasion to convert friends and members of his extended family. Only later, after his religion had won a sufficient number of converts, did he launch an armed struggle against non-Muslims. Beginning in 622, the armies of Islam set out to conquer pagan Arab tribes and Jewish tribes living around Mecca and Medina in the Saudi Peninsula. For the next century, the armies of Islam rode from victory to victory in a series of brilliant battles that destroyed every army and city that resisted their invasion. Islam conquered a staggering number of ancient kingdoms and besieged cities from India's Ganges River to the Pyrenees Mountains in the north of the Spanish Peninsula. No other religion has expanded as rapidly as did Islam after the death of Muhammad the prophet in 632.

While Islamic culture originated with Muhammad and his followers in the Arabian Peninsula, the faith of the prophet expanded by armed conquest throughout the formerly Christian populations of North Africa, the Spanish Peninsula, Turkey, and then to the east, across Asia, India, and as far as Indonesia and Malaysia in Southeast Asia. As a result of this series of military conquests, Islam absorbed numerous cultures and former civilizations that were quite distinct from its Arab tribal origins.

## THE WARRIOR PROPHET

Muhammad, the prophet who founded Islam, came from a line of fierce warriors. Muhammad's grandfather, Abul-Motalleb,[2] gained great fame throughout Arabia by defeating the princes and occupying armies of Ethiopia. Abul-Motalleb's favorite and youngest son, Abdullah, married a beautiful woman named Amina. She gave birth to a son, Muhammad, who would change the face of the world. Tragically, Abdullah died, leaving his young son with a very small bequest of five camels and an Ethiopian slave girl. When Amina died shortly afterward, the young boy was given for safe-keeping to his aged grandfather, Abul-Motalleb. Later on, Muhammad was given to his uncle, Abu-Taleb,[3] a respected trader and prince of Mecca, who held the pagan religious title of pontiff of the temple.[4] Muhammad learned from his uncle the art of trading as well as the art of war—from the constant skirmishes between the tribes and from defending the trade routes against bandits.

Muhammad gained greater stature at age twenty-five when a woman named Kadijah, the wealthy widow of a trader, acquired his services to oversee her large trading company. It wasn't long before Kadijah (who was twice his age) married Muhammad. As a young man, he attained respect and economic security as a major merchant in Mecca. Always a serious and contemplative man who faithfully worshiped the pagan idols in Mecca, Muhammad now had the financial independence to devote his life to charity, fasting, prayer, and meditation in the desert and in the caves of Mount Hara. After fifteen years, in 610, Muhammad announced to a small group of followers that he was the final prophet of God and had received a new revelation of truth that superseded the previous revelations recorded in the Jewish Bible (the *Tanach*) and the Christian New Testament. He explained that his Koran was the original revelation of God and that the Bible of both the Christians and Jews had been corrupted and changed from the original Koranic revelation of God.

It is astonishing that Muhammad expected Arab pagans, Christians, and Jews to abandon their religious practices in favor of something completely new. Skeptical listeners demanded that he authenticate his new "revelation" with divine miracles, as performed by the prophets of Judaism and Christianity. Muhammad acknowledged that he could not produce supernatural miracles or prophecies. However, he claimed that the miracles of the Bible had failed to convince people, and he appealed to the beauty of the teachings of the Koran in his attempt to win converts. But after three years of teaching at Mecca, only fourteen converts had been convinced to abandon paganism and adopt Islam.

## THE INTRODUCTION OF JIHAD

The Koreish tribe—the dominant pagan group governing the area around Mecca—violently resisted this new religious teaching that sought to destroy the idols surrounding the Kaaba in Mecca. By 622 the pressures and assassination plots became too threatening, and Muhammad, his friend Abu-Bakr, and his small group of converts fled at night to Medina. The flight from Mecca became known as the Hijra. The new religion continued to face great opposition, especially from the tribe of Koreish, but eventually a fairly large group of converts joined Muhammad at Medina.

Initially, he declared that men and women were free to believe whatever they wished regarding God. In the early passages of the Koran the following words appear: "Let there be no violence in religion" (Sura 2:256).

Muhammad had preached a faith of persuasion for thirteen years (610–22) with only limited success and against much opposition. In Medina, he changed his teaching entirely. He revealed that the angel Gabriel had given him a divine command to expand Islam through jihad (holy war), using the sword and flame to defeat all who refused to worship Allah.

According to the hadith commentaries of the teaching of the prophet Muhammad, he reframed his teaching: "The sword is the key of heaven and of hell; a drop of blood shed in the cause of God, a night spent under arms, is of more avail than two months of fasting and prayer: whosoever falls in battle his sins are forgiven."[5] Muhammad also wrote: "And when the months wherein ye are not allowed to attack them shall be past, kill the idolaters wheresoever ye shall find them, and take them prisoners, and besiege them, and lay wait for them in every convenient place" (Sura 9:5).

Following stunning military victories over the larger army of Koreish at the valley of Bedar in AD 624 and at Ohud in 625, the armies of Muhammad attacked and decimated one enemy after another. Then Muhammad massacred the Jewish tribes that for centuries had lived in peace in Arabia. When the Jews refused to abandon their faith in favor of Islam, Muhammad declared war on them and used their captured wealth to provision his growing armies.

Within two years his military strength was great enough to allow Muhammad to reenter Mecca, violating the terms of a ten-year truce he had signed with the Koreish tribe. Now that he had a superior military force, Muhammad broke his truce and overwhelmed the Koreish army.

It is worth noting that the word *peace* as we understand it does not exist in Arabic. Their concept of peace is a limited truce that is honored temporarily—until the forces of Islam become strong enough to destroy their enemy. Muhammad declared in the Koran that Muslims can sign only a limited truce with a stronger enemy, for a maximum term of ten years.

However, as soon as the Islamic forces gain strength or the situation otherwise changes in their favor, they are free to break the truce and attack their enemy without warning (see Sura 48).

## THE FIVE PILLARS OF ISLAM

The Islamic faith revolves around the concept of submission to Allah, which is expressed through Arkan-al-Islam, the five "pillars of Islam." These requirements are faith, prayer, fasting, giving alms, and the pilgrimage to Mecca. Sunni Islam speaks specifically of the five pillars, and Shi'ite Muslims follow the same fundamental religious pattern.[6]

### Faith (Iman)

"There is no god but Allah, and Muhammad is His messenger." This primary declaration of faith is known as the Shahadah, a prayer that all Muslims declare. The only purpose in life for a devout Muslim is to serve Allah by following the teachings and practices of the prophet Muhammad. The implicit faith of Muslims is expressed in this quotation from the Koran: "Mohammed is not the father of any man among you; but the apostle of GOD, and the seal of the prophets: and GOD knoweth all things" (Sura 33:40).

### Prayer (Salah)

Obligatory prayers are performed five times every day. The Koran teaches that these prayers provide a direct link between the worshiper and Allah. Islam has no religious hierarchy, so prayers said in a mosque are led by a religiously learned person who knows the Koran and is respected by the congregation. The five daily prayers are recited at dawn, midday, late afternoon, sunset, and nightfall. It is essential that during prayer the faithful face toward the holy city of Mecca. The prayers are preceded by a ceremonial cleansing (ablution) with water, or sand if water is not available. The five times of prayer provide a religious cycle or rhythm to the day. The prayers are memorized and recited in Arabic (considered the holy language of the Koran), whether or not the Muslim understands the language.

### Fasting (Sawm)

During the ninth month of the Islamic lunar year, Ramadan, Muslims (teenaged and older) must abstain from drink, food, and intimate relations from dawn until sundown. Fasting is focused on self-purification and self-restraint, which lead to a greater awareness of the presence of Allah.

### Giving Alms (Zakah)

A fourth duty of faithful Muslims is the giving of alms to those in need. Each year every Muslim is to calculate the amount to be given to those less fortunate, which should equal 2.5 percent of what he has in hand in excess of the funds required to meet the legitimate needs of his family.

### The Pilgrimage to Mecca (the Hajj)

Once during their lifetime, Muslims are obligated to participate in a pilgrimage to Mecca if they are physically and financially able. Millions of Muslims from almost every nation complete such a pilgrimage every year. The annual hajj occurs in Zul Hijjah, the twelfth month of the Islamic year. Pilgrims are required to wear simple garments to avoid distinctions of class and national culture. The religious rites associated with the hajj include circling the Kaaba seven times and traveling seven times between the hills of Safa and Marwa. Later the pilgrims congregate on the large plain of 'Arafat in the desert outside Mecca, where they join in prayer for Allah's forgiveness of their sins. At the end of the hajj, they hold a festival, called Id al-Adha, which is celebrated with prayers and the exchange of gifts.

### The Sixth Pillar

These five requirements—faith, prayer, fasting, almsgiving, and the pilgrimage to Mecca—are the historic pillars of Islam. But for many Muslims, there is an essential sixth pillar of the faith. That pillar is jihad, or holy war, and in our day it is taking on greater importance.

What is it about this sixth pillar that captures the imagination and fuels the passion of so many Muslims? We will look at the answers to that question in the next chapter.

# THE SIXTH PILLAR
# OF ISLAM—JIHAD

*How Holy War Gained Unrivaled Prominence*

In much of the Muslim world, a sixth religious requirement completes the essentials of Islam: jihad. While jihad, meaning "struggle" or "holy war," is not accorded this lofty status by all Muslims, in belief and practice, jihad has always held a central place in Islam. And in our day, it is taking on much greater importance.

This is not alarmist rhetoric; it is borne out by the writings and statements of prominent Muslims. Some Muslims, including most who belong to the Khawarij sect, teach that jihad is, in fact, the sixth pillar of Islam. While the demand for continuous jihad against nonbelievers is not emphasized by the majority of Muslim scholars, those who support Islamic extremism now teach the doctrine of holy war to millions of Muslim students—many of whom ultimately become terrorists and suicide bombers. Followers of the extremist jihad philosophy have joined the ranks of al Qaeda and associated terrorist groups whose numbers are now estimated to include as many as 120,000 dedicated and trained terrorists.

## THE WEST'S VIEW OF JIHAD

Although some observers in the West acknowledge the violent and totalitarian nature of the global jihad movement, many commentators insist that the Islamic world is not committed to holy war. Other scholars claim that the impulse to engage in jihad is nothing more than an understandable defensive response. They ask, How else are Muslim nations to react to Western cultural, religious, and military provocations? Such assessments define jihad as the use of military force solely in defense of Islam.

A typical Western analysis is that the spirit and practice of jihad were reawakened after the 1948 birth of the modern Jewish state in the midst of the Arab Middle East. Other commonly cited precursors include foreign military threats, the economic domination of Islamic nations by Western world powers, U.S. support for Israel, the U.S. military domination of the Persian Gulf, and pervasive Western cultural imperialism. However, these analyses overlook fourteen centuries of Muslim history.

The primary application of jihad is the Muslim use of military force (including terrorism) to defeat all non-Muslim "infidels" and to consolidate surrounding territory under totalitarian Islamic control. In past centuries, jihads were not waged in response to a military invasion by a Western power. Muslim fundamentalists during the nineteenth and early twentieth centuries attacked both non-Muslims and moderate Muslim neighbors who refused to embrace the extremist views. In the 1820s and 1830s, Padri Islamists in West Sumatra attacked moderate Muslims who were accused of paganism. In the 1860s, an extremist Muslim imam launched a murderous jihad against Sikhs and other non-Muslim groups living in the Punjab region of India.[1] After World War I, Muslim terrorists launched repeated massacres in south India, including the forced conversions of hundreds of thousands of Hindus to Islam and the desecration of many Hindu temples.

If you follow international news, you know that today non-Muslims are under the constant threat of attack from Islamic extremists throughout the Middle East, West Africa, and Indonesia. Jihad is a continuing threat that becomes active when extremist Islamic leaders live in proximity to non-Muslims or even moderate Muslims and feel they have enough support to launch attacks against "enemy" targets.

## THE HISTORY OF JIHAD

The modern-day war on terror did not commence with the attack on the World Trade Center and the Pentagon on September 11, 2001. And it will not end when Iraq becomes a self-governing, self-policing nation. To understand the scope and necessity of the war on terror, we must first understand the motives and religious worldview of Muslim extremists. If you read the statements issued by a wide variety of Muslim terrorists and fundamentalist religious leaders, you will realize that their mind-set is fixed in the seventh century, when Muhammad launched the most extraordinary and violent religious war in history. The Koran urges Islamic believers to embrace the practice of jihad in their continuous attempts to defeat the Judeo-Christian civilization of the West. Christian author Michael Youssef wrote about the centrality of jihad in his book *America, Oil, & the Islamic Mind:* "Unlike other religions, Islam has as one of its most basic tenets the endless pursuit of jihad, the ongoing holy war being fought for conversion and domination, and all true Muslims believe in it and pursue it to some extent or another."[2]

### The First Great Jihad
For one hundred years, beginning in AD 632, the vast cavalry armies of Muhammad's successors defeated all the Christian and pagan armies they encountered, from the Pyrenees in northern Spain to the banks of the Ganges River in India—thousands of miles to the east. Muslims think of this explosion of the Islamic religion as the First Great Jihad, the successful

holy war that used the power of the sword to subdue all non-Muslim neighbors. The forces of Islam defeated the armies of North Africa, the Middle East, Persia, and India.

In the centuries before Muhammad, the Western Roman Empire succumbed to a series of invasions from the Goths and other forces, which set the stage for the victories of the fast-moving armies of the Islamic caliphate. Meanwhile, the Eastern Roman (Byzantine) Empire based in Constantinople was desperately attempting to maintain its power and glory as the remnant of the ancient Roman Empire. The Byzantine Empire was able to muster its military power to resist the armies of the prophet for many centuries before it was ultimately defeated through treachery in 1453.

The advance of the First Great Jihad into Europe was repelled at the seven-day battle of Tours in Gaul (France) in the summer of 732. The Christian army led by Prince Charles Martel defeated the much larger Islamic army led by the Arab general Abd er Rahman.

The undefeated Muslim general had invaded Europe with more than one hundred thousand veteran soldiers and a superb Berber cavalry. Abd er Rahman was one of the ablest and most renowned Arab commanders, having conquered North Africa and Spain and governing the Iberian Peninsula as caliph. After a century of victories, the Arab army traveled with an immense number of relatives and servants and with vast treasure in the hope of establishing homes in the conquered cities of Europe.

The Arab army savagely attacked the population of Tours, which angered the troops of Charles Martel. Even though the Arab army had the advantage of an overwhelming military force, it lost the battle. In the battle's final stages, Abd er Rahman was killed. The general's death led to a collapse of the Arab army's confidence and precipitated a massive retreat. Contemporary historical accounts recorded by Christian monks report that as many as 375,000 Arab soldiers were killed (probably an exaggeration), with the deaths of only a few thousand Christian soldiers from Martel's army of perhaps 75,000 veteran troops.

While we need to discount the possibly exaggerated numbers found in medieval accounts, the evidence from chroniclers from both sides of the battle suggests a massive Christian victory. Many historians agree that had Martel failed to turn back the invading force, Islam would almost certainly have conquered Europe, and the subsequent history of Western civilization would have been radically different. Edward Gibbon, author of *The Decline and Fall of the Roman Empire,* described the battle of Tours as "the events that rescued our ancestors of Britain, and our neighbors of Gaul, from the civil and religious yoke of the Koran."[3] The historian Friedrich von Schlegel wrote, "The arm of Charles Martel saved and delivered the Christian nations of the West from the deadly grasp of all-destroying Islam."[4] (In 1492, seven centuries after the battle of Tours, the armies of Islam were finally driven out of Spain in the battle of Granada.)

In their deeply felt sense of destiny and fatalism, the Muslims reluctantly accepted that Allah at that time had not given them the anticipated victory over the hated Christians of western Europe.[5]

## The Second Great Jihad

Nearly one thousand years after the First Great Jihad, the Islamic armies of the Ottoman Empire launched another invasion of western Europe, meeting the much smaller Christian armies of Austria and Poland at the gates of Vienna. The Ottoman Turks were centered in Constantinople, the ancient capital of the Eastern Roman Empire, which was conquered in 1453. The Ottoman Empire revitalized the Islamic world with its wealth and revived military force.

In 1683, the massive Islamic army launched its last unsuccessful attempt to conquer Europe by besieging Vienna, the Christian capital of the Holy Roman Empire. The Christian army of between 100,000 and 130,000 Austrian, German, and Polish soldiers led by Polish king John Sobieski met the Muslim armies of approximately 140,000 Turkish and Tatar soldiers led by general and grand vizier Kara Mustafa. Sobieski forced Mustafa's soldiers to retreat from the gates of Vienna, and the Polish heavy cavalry charged the Turkish general's forces and routed them.

In the sixteen years that followed the failed siege of Vienna, the Christian armies drove the Turkish armies south of the Danube River, and the Ottomans never returned. The Christian victory destroyed the territorial ambitions of the Ottoman Turks, and Islam rapidly retreated into a series of small sheikhdoms, principalities, and nomadic Arab tribes throughout the deserts of the Middle East.

In the Treaty of Karlowitz, the Ottoman Turks surrendered vast amounts of territory in eastern Europe. (While the Islamic forces had been repelled at Tours hundreds of years earlier, the armies of Islam had conquered much of eastern Europe and the eastern Mediterranean.) Under the terms of the treaty, the Ottoman Empire ceded territory in Hungary, Dalmatia, Transylvania, Slavonia, and Morea. As a result of the withdrawal of the Ottoman Empire from eastern Europe, the Christian Hapsburgs became the dominant military and political power in southeastern Europe.

Bernard Lewis wrote about the long-range effect of this second great defeat: "For the past three hundred years since the failure of the second Turkish siege of Vienna in 1683 and the rise of the European colonial empires in Asia and Africa, Islam has been on the defensive."[6]

Most people in the Islamic world accepted the military disaster at the gates of Vienna as a sign that Allah would not grant them victory over the Christian West at that time. However, they still believed the day would arrive when total victory would be theirs and their dream of a global Islamic caliphate would be realized. In the meantime, the Muslim world entered a period of waiting quietly until the time for a successful jihad would finally arise.

### The Third Great Jihad

In our generation, the Third Great Jihad has been launched against both the State of Israel and the Judeo-Christian civilization of Europe and North America. Throughout the Islamic world, teachers and religious leaders preach the necessity of waging holy war against the West. This focus on jihad takes the place of analyzing and critiquing Muslim society for its failure to improve the lives and living conditions of its people. In place of self-assessment, there is a growing tendency to blame their internal problems and failures on the West and Israel.

The Third Great Jihad has its roots in the early 1800s with a revival of extreme fundamentalist Islam called Wahhabiism in Saudi Arabia. This movement attacked all Western elements that influenced Arab society. Wahhabiism rose to political and religious power under the ruling house of Saud, and with enormous financial assistance, it exported its extremist anti-Western (and anti-Christian and anti-Jewish) teaching to mosques through-out the world. It is estimated that as many as 80 percent of the mosques and imams in Europe, North America, and South America are supported financially by the Saudi government and private Saudi citizens.[7]

Wahhabiism demands the complete rejection and total destruction of anything that is not based on the original Koranic teachings of Muhammad. This extreme fundamentalist teaching finds expression in the repression of women, children, and any Muslims who are more moderate than the Taliban in Afghanistan and the followers of Ayatollah Ruhollah Khomeini in Iran.

On March 31, 1979, Khomeini's Islamic revolution overthrew the shah of Iran and created the world's first extremist Islamic state. As a result, Iran is dedicated to the utter destruction of Israel, Europe, and America. Khomeini proclaimed April 1, 1979, as the "first day of God's government."[8] With the establishment of the Islamic Republic of Iran, Khomeini became the supreme leader (Vali-e Faqeeh). He believed that he was a divinely appointed avenger against the Western nations for the humiliations that the West had inflicted on the Muslims of the Middle East in the previous hundred years. Fanatical Islamic students in Iran seized the U.S. embassy and held fifty-two American diplomatic personnel hostage for more than a year. Ronald Reagan, after he was elected president in 1980, brought pressure to bear on Khomeini's regime, and the hostages were released on Reagan's inauguration day.

During the decade of Khomeini's brutal rule over Iran, his government turned out to be as ruthless as the shah's secret police had been. Thousands of critics were killed while Khomeini's secret police and members of the Revolutionary Guard wiped out a growing rebellion from the nonreligious left. He overturned the government offices by appointing Islamic clerics who would do his will. He purged the military and security service of all non-Islamic influence and rebuilt them with loyal Muslims willing to adhere to the goal of the Islamic Revolution to eliminate the West.[9]

## VIOLENT OPPOSITION TO WESTERN INFLUENCE

In the centuries following the discovery of America in 1492, the western European powers rapidly conquered a vast amount of the world through their superior navigational abilities and advanced technology (including military technology), overwhelming other civilizations. According to Samuel Huntington in his book *The Clash of Civilizations and the Remaking of World Order*, the West "controlled 35 percent of the earth's land surface in 1800, 67 percent in 1878, and 84 percent in 1914.… The West won the world not by the superiority of its ideas or values or religion (to which few members of other civilizations were converted) but rather by its superiority in applying organized violence. Westerners often forget this fact; non-Westerners never do."[10]

Nations that feel they have been subjugated by the West—either militarily or ideologically—have long memories. After an Islamic revolution ousted the shah of Iran and ended his attempts to modernize the country, Khomeini instilled in the country his own deep hatred for Israel and the United States. As a result, the Third Great Jihad gained a strong base of operations in and the massive oil wealth of the Persian Gulf. A primary goal is the elimination of Western values of political and religious freedom and the replacement of all secular and democratic national leadership with Muslim-led governments that will rule according to strict Islamic standards.

The long-term strategy of the Third Great Jihad is built around three strategic goals. The first is to force the withdrawal of all U.S. military forces from the Middle East. While it's true that America has withdrawn its forces from the Saudi Peninsula, it has established a group of military bases throughout the Middle East and Asia that extend the reach of the U.S. military throughout the Islamic and Arab world.

Islamic extremists support the establishment of the United Nations as the major arbiter of all negotiations regarding the Middle East. The hope is that with the U.N. brokering such arrangements, the complete withdrawal of Western military forces from all Islamic dominated countries will more quickly become a reality.

The second goal of the Third Great Jihad is for Islamic leaders to take control of the oil wealth possessed by Muslim countries, which accounts for as much as 75 percent of the world's known petroleum reserves.

The third goal is to develop and use nuclear, chemical, and biological weapons to annihilate the enemies of Islam. We will look at this goal in greater detail in a later chapter.

## Extremist Islam and Jihad

In 1998 Sheikh Muhammad al-Hanooti, a member of the Fiqh Council of North America (FCNA), an American-Arab Islamic council of religious scholars, publicly called for the launching of jihad against the United States and the United Kingdom. The sheikh declared, "Allah will curse the Americans and British." He also stated, "The curse of Allah will become true on the infidel Jews and on the tyrannical Americans."[11] Al-Hanooti served on the board of the Islamic Association for Palestine (IAP), which is closely linked to the terrorist group Hamas. The U.S. Immigration and Naturalization Service noted in a 2002 memo that the IAP is "part of Hamas' propaganda apparatus."[12]

On July 28, 2005, the Fiqh Council of North America (FCNA) and the Council on American-Islamic Relations (CAIR), Muslim groups based in the United States, announced that for the first time they had issued a fatwa (religious decree) that condemned terrorism. However, the fatwa does not specifically condemn the extremist jihad ideology that has motivated Islamic terrorism. Further, the fatwa fails to renounce the Islamic jihadist culture that has permeated up to 80 percent of the mosques throughout the world and infected millions of young Muslims in both the West and the East. Significantly, the fatwa doesn't condemn any specific Islamic group or leader.[13]

### The Meaning of Islamism

There is a significant difference between moderate Muslims and Islamists. The word *Islamism* is used to identify a set of political ideologies derived from extremely conservative and fundamentalist Islamic views that endorse global jihad to violently impose an Islamic system of law and way of life. This viewpoint declares that Islam is not simply a religion but encompasses a political system that must determine the legal, economic, and social rules of every nation. Islamist groups (also known as Islamic fundamentalists or extremists) want to violently conquer and transform every nation in the world by imposing *shari'ah*—strict Islamic law based on the Koran and the hadith (the Muslim commentary on the Koran). Following the September 11, 2001, attacks in New York City and Washington DC, some Islamist movements have become targets in the international war on terror.

Throughout the last century, socialism and pan-Arab nationalism became major political forces within the decolonized Arab and Islamic nations. However, the socialist and military governments of the Arab nations were unable to raise the standard of living and quality of life of their populations, despite more than a trillion dollars in oil and natural gas revenues since World War II. Petroleum revenues were largely wasted on prestigious buildings, obsolete armaments, and massive corruption. Very little was invested in building infrastructure, educating the next generation, or diversifying national economies in preparation for the inevitable day when oil revenues would decrease significantly.

In the early 1990s, the Soviet communist system collapsed and, with it, Soviet support of Arab nations. Economic stagnation followed in the Islamic world. Many Muslims began searching for new ways to recover the lost glories. There is an enormous nostalgia in the Arab world for the past centuries of conquest, when the armies of Muhammad's successors conquered every nation from Spain to India.

Many Muslims have chosen to blame the influx of Western and "foreign" ideas for the economic failures of Islamic societies. Millions have embraced a romantic notion of a return to the fundamentalist principles of seventh-century Islam as the only cure for the ills of modern Islamic society. A constantly repeated theme throughout the Islamic world is that Muslims are being persecuted by the Christian West, Israel, other infidels, and moderate Muslim governments that refuse to adopt strict shari'ah law.

## THE RISE OF EXTREME ISLAM

After centuries of relative passivity while the West rose to global predominance militarily, economically, and politically, the radical Islamic world has now awakened. Three major factors are responsible for this awakening: (1) a massive increase in the world's Muslim population, with an enormous portion of that population being young adults; (2) an unprecedented increase in wealth derived from oil revenues; and (3) the rise of a number of charismatic Islamic leaders. In 1979, Muslim cleric Ayatollah Khomeini created the world's first Islamic republic in Iran. The government he established is dedicated to leading the entire globe to a totalitarian Islamic caliphate. Meanwhile, Osama bin Laden has articulated the dream of the complete conquest of Western culture and the defeat of the major superpowers, including Russia and the United States.

The exploding populations of Muslim nations have created massive destabilization as enormous numbers of unemployed or underemployed youth seek a place to belong. Many of them have been displaced from rural villages and are searching not only for work but also for new identities that will allow them to understand who they are and what roles they should play. Economically and socially displaced young men are vulnerable to extremist Islamic teachers who tell them that the problems faced by the Islamic world are the fault of the West and the Jews. In addition, untold numbers of young Muslim adults accept that the solution to their problems lies in engaging in violent jihad against all infidels as well as moderate, "apostate" Muslims who are not dedicated to a violent Islamic victory over the West.

Between 1919 (the end of the Ottoman Empire) and 1979 (the birth of the Islamic Republic of Iran), the world experienced relative peace between Islam and the West. Sixty years of peaceful coexistence led many people to consider that to be the normal state of affairs. But even a cursory review of the last fourteen centuries, beginning with the birth of Islam in 622, reveals that most of those years were characterized by a series of violent upheavals and wars. Naturally, even the last six decades were interspersed with violent conflicts in the Middle East between Islam and the new State of Israel, as well as conflicts between Islamic Pakistan and Hindu India. But today, nearly thirty years into the Third Great Jihad, the world is witnessing a return to the holy war that Muhammad authorized against all non-Muslims.

Scholar Bernard Lewis wrote in 1990:

For a long time now there has been a rising tide of rebellion against this Western paramountcy, and a desire to reassert Muslim values and restore Muslim greatness. The Muslim has suffered successive stages of defeat. The first was his loss of domination in the world, to the advancing power of Russia and the West. The second was the undermining of his authority in his own country, through an invasion of foreign ideas and laws and ways of life and sometimes even foreign rulers or settlers, and the enfranchisement of native non-Muslim elements. The third—the last straw—was the challenge to his mastery in his own house, from emancipated women and rebellious children. It was too much to endure, and the outbreak of rage against these alien, infidel, and incomprehensible forces that had subverted his dominance, disrupted his society, and finally violated the sanctuary of his home was inevitable.[14]

## THE WEST'S ADVANTAGE OVER EXTREME ISLAM

With the West now engaged in a long-term power struggle with a reinvigorated, insurgent Islam, it is important to recognize that the West possesses a staggering advantage over the forces of Islam, including:

- The West has superior military technology, dominates the aerospace industry and space exploration, and has vital satellite surveillance.
- The West operates military bases in more than one hundred nations, which gives the United States and its allies the ability to mobilize forces anywhere in the world.
- The West dominates the world economy and the global financial system, including capital markets.
- The West controls the air and sea lanes essential to the flow of economic goods, including energy resources that are vital to the survival of the Western nations.
- Aside from the Islamic world's dominance in oil and gas reserves, it has few natural resources and has generally squandered the trillion-plus U.S. dollars that Muslim OPEC nations have earned in the last eighty-five years. By and large they have not invested heavily in education or building infrastructure for a well-balanced future economy. When their oil reserves become seriously depleted in the post-2030 era, their economic prospects will be bleak.
- Despite the West's dependence on petroleum—much of it exported by Islamic OPEC nations—there remain a number of extensive oil reserves in the West, including vast oil sands in northern Alberta (minimum 300 billion barrels),[15] estimated to contain more oil than Saudi Arabia (261.7 billion barrels).[16] In addition, an enormous number of oil wells were abandoned years ago in North America, and they have accumulated a great deal of oil over the decades.[17]

In the next chapter, we will examine the renewed emphasis on expanding Islam through violent threats against and conquest of non-Muslim neighbors. Extremist Islam has reverted to the historic call to jihad, urging millions of devout Muslims to kill those who reject Islam. This development represents the greatest threat to our freedom and way of life since the darkest days of the Third Reich and the Japanese attacks on the West in the 1940s.

The new war against the West is rightly called *The Next World War* because the goal of Islamic fundamentalism is nothing less than the total destruction of Judeo-Christian democratic culture. It is vital that we realize the nature of the threat that faces our generation.

# OSAMA BIN LADEN DECLARES WAR ON THE WEST

## *The Military Threat from Radical Islam*

Several years after the devastating 2001 terrorist attacks that killed more than three thousand innocent victims in New York City, Washington DC, and Pennsylvania, Americans are still confused about the nature of the terrorists' grievances and true goals. Virtually all who attack our citizens and society identify with the extremist elements of Islam, but what is their real agenda?

It's important that we understand who the terrorists are, where they came from, and what they hope to achieve.

### OSAMA BIN LADEN—THE EMIR OF AL QAEDA

Osama bin Laden was born in 1957 in Riyadh, the capital of Saudi Arabia. He is one of fifty children fathered by Muhammad bin Laden, who became extremely wealthy by operating an enormous construction company in Saudi Arabia with branches throughout the Middle East. Muhammad bin Laden was a close friend of many Saudi princes, and his company was awarded lucrative contracts, including the rebuilding and refurbishing of sacred buildings in both Mecca and Medina, the two most holy cities in Islam.

When he was young, Osama bin Laden's life did not reflect a committed Muslim faith. After living as a wealthy Arab playboy, enjoying the flesh-pots of Beirut, Osama became seriously interested in Islam in the 1970s and undertook intense religious studies with several extremist Muslim teachers. These scholars instilled within him a love of Islam's most extreme theology and a fanatical hatred of Jews, Christians, and the Western world. One Arab journalist who had the opportunity to spend some time with bin Laden reported that he "wants to die a martyr and believes he will go to heaven."[1]

### Bin Laden in Afghanistan

After he committed to launch jihad against the enemies of Islam, Osama moved to Afghanistan in the mid-1980s to join the resistance fighters. He provided tens of millions of dollars to help organize an effective guerrilla war against the brutal Soviet occupation of Afghanistan. He occasionally fought side by side with the Afghan fighters, who eventually forced the Soviet military out of the country in 1989.

The following year Saddam Hussein's Iraqi army invaded Kuwait. The United States responded by deploying the largest Western military force ever assembled in the Middle East. More than seven hundred thousand U.S. troops trained in the deserts of Saudi Arabia to engage the Iraqi forces occupying Kuwait. Selected forces from the United Kingdom and other Western countries joined in the preparations for war. In the spring of 1991, the U.S. Air Force destroyed the Iraqi Air Force and many key Iraqi military targets in only six weeks. The Western forces rapidly overwhelmed Hussein's Republican Guard, the fourth largest army in the world at that time. Many Saudi citizens were content with the United States' protection of their nation from the threat of Iraqi attack. However, Osama was outraged by the presence of Christian and Jewish American soldiers in military bases in the deserts of his home country, the birthplace of Islam. It made no difference that U.S. soldiers were protecting Saudi Arabia from invasion by Iraq's secular army.

### Expelled from Saudi Arabia

Osama publicly criticized the policies of the Saudi royal family and, in 1994, was expelled from Saudi Arabia to Sudan. His passport and Saudi citizenship were revoked. His financial assets in Saudi Arabia were frozen. He ran the balance of his family's construction business in Sudan and East Africa for a number of years and continued to build up and direct the activities of his army of trained al Qaeda terrorists from a new headquarters in Khartoum, the capital of Sudan. His forces subsequently launched several terrorist attacks against American troops in Somalia. It is important to note that during this period bin Laden built an extensive fleet of deep-ocean tankers and other ships that later enabled him to send his operatives and weapons anywhere in the world with little chance of detection.

Facing increasing pressure from American military and intelligence operations, bin Laden traveled to Afghanistan in 1996 with hundreds of his most dedicated allies to cement an alliance with the extremist Taliban. They set up secret al Qaeda training and supply bases in a series of enormous caverns hidden deep within the rugged Afghan mountains. He solidified his partnership with the Taliban government and its leader, Muhammad Omar, whom bin Laden had befriended and supported with finances and illegal weapons. Bin Laden became the de facto finance minister of the Taliban government, charged with handling its hundreds of millions of dollars of annual revenues generated from the cultivation and export of more than 80 percent of the world's heroin.[2]

## BIN LADEN'S DECLARATION OF WAR ON AMERICA

In 1996 bin Laden issued a public declaration of war against the United States, encouraging Muslims around the globe to kill U.S. soldiers. In 1998 he issued another fatwa (a religious decree to all observant Muslims) commanding his followers to kill all Americans—soldiers or civilians (men, women, and children)—anywhere in the world. He declared that any Muslims who refused to heed his call were guilty of behaving as apostates (defined as Muslims who have forsaken the faith of their fathers).[3]

In all of bin Laden's public declarations, he repeats the first fundamental and strategic goal of al Qaeda and its allies: to expel all Americans, military and civilian, from Saudi Arabia and the entire Middle East. Bin Laden's "Declaration of War Against the Americans Occupying the Land of the Two Holy Places" declares: "The latest and the greatest of [the] aggressions, incurred by the Muslims since the death of the Prophet…is the occupation of the land of the two Holy Places—the foundation of the house of Islam, the place of the revelation, the source of the message and the place of the noble Ka'ba, the Qiblah of all Muslims—by the armies of the American Crusaders and their allies."[4]

Bin Laden founded the International Islamic Front for Jihad Against the Jews and the Crusaders, which published a fatwa that proclaimed a jihad against the Christians who conquered Muslim lands. This applies even to Spain, which was conquered fourteen centuries ago by Muslim armies and liberated by Christian armies in 1492. In February 1998 bin Laden announced that many key terrorist groups had joined an alliance between al Qaeda and the International Islamic Front for Jihad Against the Jews and Crusaders. Allied groups include the Egyptian Islamic Jihad, the Egyptian al-Gama'at al-Islamiyya, and the Harakat ul-Ansar.[5]

In May 1998 John Miller of ABC News was granted an unprecedented interview with bin Laden, in which he revealed his hatred of the Jews and Christians of the West. He claimed that holy war is essential to allow the Islamic nations to defeat the world dominated by Christian and Jewish "heretics." Terrorism against Westerners is justified, he said, because no Western citizens are innocent. He claimed that the degraded moral standards of Islam's Christian and Jewish enemies justify any terrorist atrocities.[6]

This obscene justification of blind brutality was delivered by a man who is responsible for destroying the lives of men, women, and children from many different faiths, including Islam, in numerous nations throughout the world. Bin Laden claims that the United States should be held responsible for what he calls acts of world terrorism, including the use of atomic bombs on Hiroshima and Nagasaki during World War II and the Allies' bombing of Iraq in 1991. In addition, he has used pejorative and hate-filled anti-Semitic language in his many public attacks on the Jewish people.

## BIN LADEN'S FATWA URGING JIHAD AGAINST AMERICANS

Two years after his 1996 declaration, bin Laden updated his threats against the West in a fatwa published in *Al-Quds al-'Arabi* on February 23, 1998. This fatwa by bin Laden includes the following statement: "The ruling to kill the Americans and their allies—civilians and military—is an individual duty for every Muslim who can do it in any country in which it is possible to do it, in order to liberate the al-Aqsa Mosque and the holy mosque from their grip."[7]

Bin Laden justified al Qaeda attacks against Israel based on his claims that the Jews were responsible for attacks on Arab villagers at Dir Yassin during the 1948 War of Independence and for the brutal attack by Lebanese Christian militias against Palestinians in the Sabra and Shatila refugee camps in 1982, after Israel drove the Palestine Liberation Organization (PLO) out of Lebanon.[8]

Former Saudi Arabian diplomat Abdullah bin Saad al-Otaibi stated that al Qaeda had built "well-constructed and well-equipped" subterranean chambers in Afghanistan and northwest Pakistan to protect bin Laden's terrorist groups. Hundreds of bunkers and extensive caverns were built to withstand bunker-buster smart bombs and deep-penetration cruise missiles. These bunkers are equipped with food supplies, batteries, Internet communication networks, oxygen supplies, air conditioning, and water tanks. Al-Otaibi revealed that bin Laden does not trust anyone except possibly his top aide, the leader of the Egyptian Islamic Jihad, Ayman al-Zawahiri, the technical genius behind many of the most sophisticated terrorist attacks, including the September 11, 2001, attack on the World Trade Center and the Pentagon.[9]

To avoid capture or assassination, bin Laden constantly changes his plans, his routes of travel, and the cave headquarters he occupies. He never sleeps in the same place twice. In addition, intelligence sources have reported that bin Laden arranged for a Russian plastic surgeon to alter his facial features to enable him to escape surveillance. A 1999 report from *Al Watan al Arabi,* a newspaper in Paris, described an elaborate attempt to disguise not only the features of bin Laden but also the facial features of his favorite wife and several key assistants and trusted bodyguards.[10]

## THE AL QAEDA TERRORIST ARMY

While al Qaeda ("the base") was organized by bin Laden, it includes a number of additional terrorist groups, including the Egyptian Islamic Jihad from the Middle East. In the late 1980s, bin Laden focused on assisting the mujahedin (Afghan guerrillas) who were fighting to drive the Soviet Union's invading army from their nation. Bin Laden recruited thousands of young Muslim men throughout the Middle East and other Islamic nations to join in a jihad against the Soviet "infidels."

In recognition of the danger to Western security posed by Russia's occupation of Afghanistan and its centuries-long ambition to obtain direct access to the Indian Ocean for its navy, America joined with Saudi Arabia and Pakistan in an unprecedented anti-Soviet alliance. The alliance armed the mujahedin with sophisticated communication devices and modern armaments, including hundreds of shoulder-held U.S. surface-to-air Stinger missiles. The mujahedin became adept at shooting down Russian planes and powerful Hind helicopters. Despite efforts by the CIA to buy back the unused antiaircraft missiles after the war, apparently up to five hundred of them remain in the hands of al Qaeda and associated terrorist groups.

In 1989, when the Russian army abandoned its decade-long effort to occupy Afghanistan, the victorious mujahedin forces captured the capital, Kabul. However, they proved unable to build a government that had support from the many different tribes and ambitious, independent warlords. The country descended into a deadly civil war as various generals used captured Soviet military equipment to defeat their rivals. Finally, after four years of brutal civil war, in 1994 a group of Islamic extremists known as the Taliban ("teachers of religion") gathered weapons and seized control of significant parts of the ruined nation. They quickly imposed brutal Islamic law, shari'ah, and killed anyone who rejected their extreme Islamic agenda.

Bin Laden's al Qaeda immediately set up dozens of terrorist training camps throughout Afghanistan under the protection of the Taliban. Despite repeated demands by the United States and the United Nations that the Taliban government surrender the al Qaeda terrorists known to have been involved in terrorist attacks around the world—including the 1998 American embassy bombings in Africa—the Taliban refused to surrender bin Laden or any other terrorists within its territory.

Over the years, bin Laden used his estimated $250 million inheritance from his father's estate, his control of the lucrative Afghan heroin trade, and his brilliant financial investments to build his terrorist army and support the financially destitute Taliban government. In addition, numerous Saudi millionaire businessmen and some Saudi princes contributed millions to al Qaeda to ensure that their companies and families would not become the targets of terrorist attacks.

Al Qaeda recruited tens of thousands of fundamentalists from the Muslim southern republics of the former Soviet Union and from the Middle East to be trained to join forces with Taliban troops. Until America's military victory in Afghanistan in December 2001, the Taliban, supported by both Saudi Arabia and Pakistan's Interagency Security Service (ISS), succeeded in driving the remnants of the former Afghan government's army into the far north of the country, an area comprising less than 20 percent of the nation's land.

Not everything ran smoothly for bin Laden in Afghanistan, however. Various sources revealed that a serious conflict developed between Arab terrorists from Egypt and bin Laden's fighters from Iran. In addition, many Afghans rejected the foreign domination of their nation, because many of bin Laden's al Qaeda fighters came from Pakistan, Sudan, Yemen, Chechnya, and Bosnia.

## A NEW TYPE OF WAR

The war against terrorism differs considerably from military engagements of the past. Al Qaeda and its allies operate globally in a loosely affiliated network of networks. They are decentralized, operating in virtually independent cells in which terrorists do not know terrorists in other cells. Neither do they know the leaders who direct their violent activities. Thus, if they are captured, they can't betray other cells or their leaders. Al Qaeda supports numerous terrorist groups and independent terror organizations in Afghanistan, Pakistan, the Philippines, Algeria, Eritrea, Tajikistan, Chechnya, Somalia, Yemen, Sudan, and Kashmir. Evidence accumulated over the last decade by the CIA, the FBI, Israel's Mossad, France's Sûreté, and the British MI6 reveal that al Qaeda is dedicated to meticulous, long-term, strategic planning, virtually untraceable financial transfers, incredibly secure communications, rigorous training of agents, and utterly ruthless and suicidal commitment to the destruction of its enemies.

Bin Laden has declared that al Qaeda's ultimate goals are the following:

- To force all American soldiers and civilians as well as all Western influence out of every Muslim nation, especially Saudi Arabia
- To destroy Israel militarily and through terrorist means
- To destroy every pro-Western moderate Islamic government in the Middle East
- To unite all Muslims throughout the world and set up, by force, a global Islamic nation adhering to the extreme Islamic fundamentalist rule of the first caliphs[11]

If extremist Islam wins this war, humanity would enter a nightmare of living and dying in a global religious concentration camp from which there would be no escape. Every Western democratic and Arab non-Taliban-style government would be overthrown and replaced by an extremist Islamic government. Under threat of death, all people—Christians, Jews, Muslims, Hindus, Buddhists, atheists—would be forced to submit to extremist Muslim faith and the dictatorial rule of the most radical fundamentalist Islamic regime. Even the vast majority of Muslims, who reject the fanatical interpretation of Islam taught by the Taliban and al Qaeda, would be forced to submit to their extremist rules or suffer persecution and death.

Al Qaeda repeatedly calls for the killing of any apostate Muslim and the destruction of any moderate Islamic government that rejects its demands to force the world to accept its religious beliefs. Virtually all moderate Islamic religious scholars have publicly rejected the extremist views of the Taliban and al Qaeda, which are based on the writings of two Sunni Muslim scholars—Muhammad ibn Abd al-Wahhab and Sayyid Qutb.

Muhammad ibn Abd al-Wahhab lived in Saudi Arabia in the late 1700s and declared that Islam had become corrupted in the centuries following the death of Muhammad in 632. Al-Wahhab rejected all Muslim theological teachings and customs developed during the preceding thousand years of Islamic scholarship. His extreme puritanical group succeeded in conquering the Saudi Peninsula around 1800, and his sect, known as Wahhabiism, became the dominant teaching in Saudi Arabia.

During the twentieth century, another radical Islamic scholar, Sayyid Qutb in Egypt, announced that Western civilization was the deadly enemy of Islam. Qutb attacked all the leaders of various Muslim nations because they did not submit fully to his demands for Islamic purity. He taught that all Muslims must engage in jihad to defend Islam and to purify it from Western influences.

Terrorist attacks on the West are attempts to destroy the Christian values that make our lives worthwhile. Al Qaeda will not be satisfied with any changes in policy by the West, such as a lessening of support for Israel. It desires nothing less than our complete destruction. So the West must stay the course until the scourge of Islamic terrorism is defeated. The only possible strategy when confronted by implacable evil is to marshal all of the spiritual, economic, and military forces at one's command and attack the enemy until he is utterly destroyed.

Al Qaeda benefits from massive financial and military resources, effective leadership, an abundant supply of terrorist fighters, and access to technology and weaponry—including some of the most deadly and most advanced biological, nuclear, and chemical weapons on earth. In the next chapter, we'll take a closer look at this dimension of the terrorist threat.

# AL QAEDA'S STRATEGIES AND RESOURCES

*Weaponry, Communications, and Plans for Warfare*

Western nations would pay little attention to Osama bin Laden and his followers if they were nothing more than a ragtag band of religious zealots. But with the attacks of September 11, 2001, they demonstrated their ability to plan and carry out a sophisticated plot and do real damage to their enemy. And as more information comes to light regarding their access to weapons of mass destruction (WMD), the terrorist threat becomes more immediate and much more ominous.

Since 1993 Western intelligence agencies have gathered compelling evidence that al Qaeda has devoted enormous resources to acquiring nuclear, biological, and chemical weapons. In 1998 Osama bin Laden wrote his declaration "The Nuclear Bomb of Islam," stating, "It is the duty of Muslims to prepare as much force as possible to terrorize the enemies of God."[1] Bin Laden believes it is his religious duty to acquire chemical, biological, and nuclear weapons.

Since September 11, 2001, anthrax has been sent through the mail on a number of occasions. Only a sophisticated biological weapons laboratory could produce this type of deadly airborne anthrax. Expensive milling machines break down the microscopic spores into extremely tiny particles capable of floating in the air and entering a victim's lungs. In the 1990s only three nations were known to be capable of producing weapons-grade airborne anthrax: Russia, the United States, and Iraq.

Dr. Michael Osterholm, chief of disease epidemiology at the Minnesota Department of Health, has warned the National Foundation for Infectious Disease about the danger of biological weapons. "The United States is ripe for a terrorist attack using biological weapons and is nowhere near ready for it," he stated. "There are a growing number of extremist terrorist groups and religious fanatics who believe it is now time for our 'decadent capitalist society' to come to an end, and they are actively pursuing ways to bring that about. Germ warfare is their method of choice."[2]

On ABC's *Primetime,* U.S. Army Col. David Franz admitted to interviewers Diane Sawyer and Sam Donaldson that "the likelihood of a biological attack in the U.S. is now extremely high."[3] And not only are biological attacks a likelihood, but al Qaeda also has in its possession nuclear and chemical weapons.

Former U.S. Attorney General John Ashcroft declared that the government was preparing Federal Emergency Management Agency officials in 120 major U.S. cities for the possibility of terrorist attacks. Ashcroft warned, "It is clear that American citizens are the target of choice of international terrorists. Americans comprise only about 5 percent of the world's population. However, according to State Department statistics, during the decade of the 1990s, 36 percent of all worldwide terrorist acts were directed against U.S. interests."[4]

## WHAT HAPPENED TO IRAQ'S WEAPONS OF MASS DESTRUCTION?

VX nerve gas, a WMD, is a binary gas that can be prepared only with complex chemical warfare technology, equipment, and experienced scientists. It is known from Iraqi admissions and the U.N. Special Commission

(UNSCOM) inspectors that Iraq possessed more than five hundred tons of the precursor chemicals required to produce VX-nerve-gas weapons. Iraq claimed to have destroyed these materials but never provided proof.

Israeli intelligence analysts and key players in the U.S. intelligence community, including retired U.S. Air Force Gen. James Clapper, declared that huge amounts of Iraqi WMD were transferred to Syria just before the United States invaded Iraq in March 2003. U.S. weapons inspector David Kay told Congress in testimony in 2003 that U.S. satellite surveillance revealed substantial vehicular traffic in convoys from Iraq to Syria in February and March 2003. Clapper said that the intelligence community determined the convoys contained missiles and WMD components that were banned by the U.N. Security Council.[5]

The former deputy undersecretary of defense, John A. Shaw, revealed what actually happened to Iraq's missing weapons of mass destruction. "The short answer to the question of where the WMDs Saddam bought from the Russians went was that they went to Syria and Lebanon.... They were moved by Russian Spetsnaz units out of uniform, that were specifically sent to Iraq to move the weaponry and eradicate any evidence."[6]

During the breakup of the Soviet Union in 1989 and 1990, Russia repeatedly used this type of "emergency exit" planned removal of WMD and other sophisticated military equipment from former Warsaw Pact allies in Eastern Europe, as well as from former Soviet republics such as the Ukraine and Kazakstan. A variety of respected sources, including Shaw and Saddam Hussein's former top general, Georges Sada, have confirmed that Russian Spetsnaz troops coordinated the removal of Iraq's WMD to Syria by large truck convoys and aircraft in the period just before the invasion of Iraq in April 2003.[7]

The question that will occur to most readers is why the Bush Administration endured countless attacks on the credibility of its prewar claims about Iraq's WMD and never publicly revealed the significant evidence that points to the removal of these weapons to Syria. According to both Shaw and Sada, the Bush administration's desire to protect Russia from international embarrassment motivated it to suppress this intelligence in the hope that Russia would assist America in limiting Iran's and North Korea's plans to achieve a nuclear warhead.

## A THWARTED NERVE-GAS ATTACK

It is known that al Qaeda terrorists planned a devastating VX-nerve-gas attack on the headquarters of Jordan's intelligence agency. The attack could have killed as many as twenty thousand people in the center of Amman, according to Jordanian officials.[8]

The attempted nerve-gas attack, with the weapons and terrorists entering Jordan from Syria, links Iraq not only with the production of banned weapons but also with al Qaeda. One of the concerns of those who argued for the need to overthrow Hussein's regime was that he not only had developed WMD but that he would transfer them to Islamic terrorists to use in attacks on Western allies, including moderate Muslim governments such as Jordan.[9] Jordanian officials claim that the arrested suspects confessed to a plan to detonate a chemical (VX nerve gas) bomb on the Amman headquarters of the intelligence services. The terrorists admitted as well that the planner was Abu Musab al-Zarqawi, the leader of al Qaeda in Iraq.

A Jordanian official told the Agence France-Presse (AFP) news agency: "We found primary materials to make a chemical bomb which, if it had exploded, would have made nearly 20,000 deaths…in an area of one square kilometre." Another al Qaeda operation was planning to use "deadly gas against the US embassy and the prime minister's office in Amman…and other public buildings in Jordan."[10]

## BIN LADEN HAS ACQUIRED NUCLEAR WEAPONS

Reports from intelligence agencies—based on captured documents and interrogations of defectors, captured terrorists, and senior-level al Qaeda operatives—confirm that Osama bin Laden plans to attack a series of American and possibly European cities with suitcase-size nuclear devices. These dirty bombs were acquired from the remnants of the former Soviet Union in the years following the collapse of the USSR.[11]

Jamal al-Fadi, a senior representative of bin Laden's group, met with a Sudanese army commander in Khartoum to arrange the purchase, at the price of $1.7 million, of a lead, cylindrical container holding enriched South African uranium.[12]

While building a nuclear-fission bomb is beyond bin Laden's capacity, the FBI and the CIA have stated that the acquisition or development by terrorists of a nuclear radiation device, or dirty bomb, is quite probable. This type of low-technology nuclear device uses radioactive nuclear material (from a reactor or medical laboratory) packed around conventional explosives. It could kill thousands of victims immediately and thousands more from radiation exposure after the attack. Depending on the size of the bomb, such a weapon might leave enough radioactive residue to contaminate ten city blocks, leaving them uninhabitable for a century or more. Western intelligence sources have reported that the al Qaeda network possesses nuclear materials that could be used in a dirty bomb.[13]

Gen. Aleksandr Lebed, the former Russian national security advisor, claimed that the KGB had manufactured hundreds of suitcase-size nuclear weapons during the late 1970s to be used by Spetsnaz special forces soldiers against the West. These deadly weapons were designed to appear as normal suitcases and to be carried into a European or North American city and detonated by a Russian operative. Lebed announced that more than one hundred of the suitcase-size, one-kiloton bombs (equal to one thousand tons of TNT, which could destroy a city center and kill up to a hundred thousand people) were still unaccounted for.[14]

While several senior Russian defense officials have denied the existence of the suitcase bombs, on October 2, 1997, Aleksey Yablokov, a senior advisor to former Russian president Boris Yeltsin, confirmed Lebed's warnings when he told a U.S. congressional subcommittee that he was "absolutely sure" that hundreds of suitcase-size nuclear devices were developed by the KGB during the 1970s.[15]

The late General Lebed indicated that the suitcase devices were compact nuclear weapons (twenty-four by sixteen by eight inches) and were distributed to special Soviet army intelligence units known as the Main Intelligence Directorate, or the GRU. The available information suggests that the smallest likely nuclear explosive device would be a critical mass of uranium 235 or plutonium approximately four inches across and weighing at least twenty-three pounds. In May 1997 Lebed told a delegation of U.S. congressmen that his research indicated that eighty-four of the one-kiloton bombs were still missing.[16] While some commentators have speculated that these decades-old nuclear weapons may no longer be reliable, other nuclear experts, such as Carey Sublette of Military Intelligence Network (MILNET), report that it is very unlikely these devices would be degraded to the point that they would not function.[17]

Reports appeared in Russia during October 1997 that Dzhokhar Dudayev, the leader of the Chechen separatist forces, may have purchased or stolen several Russian tactical, nuclear weapons. Lebed indicated to the United States that reports of Chechen terrorists acquiring several "suitcase nuclear weapons" had motivated the Russian Security Council to begin its investigation of the whereabouts of these deadly weapons.[18]

In the book *Bin Laden: The Man Who Declared War on America*, counterterrorism expert Yossef Bodansky reported that Chechen rebels arranged to sell to al Qaeda suitcase nuclear bombs acquired from Russia and the former Soviet republics of Ukraine, Kazakhstan, and Turkmenistan during the late 1990s. Bodansky claims that, according to Russian and Arab intelligence sources, the Chechens were paid thirty million dollars plus two tons of pure Afghan heroin (worth up to seven hundred million dollars in street prices) in exchange for several suitcase nuclear weapons.[19]

In late September 2001 it was determined that bin Laden possessed at least one Russian suitcase nuclear weapon. Israeli security forces arrested a Pakistani terrorist linked to al Qaeda as he attempted to enter Israel from Palestinian Authority territory at the border checkpoint at Ramallah. U.S. government officials acknowledged that the terrorist had been armed with a backpack radiological nuclear explosive and that he had been arrested while traveling toward an Israeli target (probably Tel Aviv, Israel's largest city).[20] That disturbing report was posted on the Internet on October 14, 2001, by Richard Sale, a United Press International (UPI) reporter. Several intelligence sources in Great Britain and Israel confirmed during private interviews with this author that the Pakistani terrorist had been arrested in possession of a nuclear device. The U.S. government official told UPI's Sale that the terrorist probably entered Israel from Lebanon and traveled through Ramallah.

Israeli intelligence authorities immediately sent this information to President George W. Bush, and a top-secret report about the terrorist's possession of a dirty atomic bomb was circulated among U.S. Cabinet members.[21] The U.S. and Israeli governments decided against releasing this information to a wide audience for fear it would cause panic if the public knew about the dangers of nuclear suitcase bombs when there was already widespread fear of anthrax attacks.

In addition to the acquisition of suitcase-size nuclear weapons from Russia, there is evidence that during the late 1970s the KGB positioned a number of secret weapon depots in Western Europe and the United States. Each of these secret depots contained several small nuclear devices that Russian Spetsnaz agents could detonate within Europe and America. This would have allowed Russia to devastate critical military command and control centers that are vital to Western defenses against military attacks. While this strategy violated numerous arms treaties, the plan would have enabled the Soviets to wipe out the major economic, military, and communication centers of the West without bombers or missiles that would have immediately identified the nation that launched the attack.

But when the Soviet Union fell apart, other political elements were able to offer staggering amounts of money to former KGB and Spetsnaz officers to reveal the locations of the nuclear weapon depots and the bombs' launch codes.[22]

If these nuclear weapons are in the hands of terrorists, they could be used with devastating effects. Only two factors could mitigate their effectiveness. First, the radioactive material in the weapons decays when the weapons are not properly maintained. Second, many of the weapons' complex codes could not be obtained or breached.

According to Western intelligence sources, the existing nuclear devices are relatively small (from two to ten kilotons). One analyst points out, "To place such an atomic device in context, the American Hiroshima nuclear weapon that killed between 80,000 and 100,000 Japanese civilians and soldiers on August 6, 1945, had a yield of 10 kilotons and destroyed the center of that city, leaving tens of thousands to die of burns and cancers in the years and decades that followed."[23]

Paul L. Williams, a journalist and a former FBI consultant on terrorism, uncovered a long-term al Qaeda strategy that included a nuclear attack on American targets long before the 2001 attacks in New York and Washington DC. In the days following 9/11, the leader of the Taliban, Mullah Omar, who was providing protection and communications at that time for bin Laden, revealed in an interview with the BBC that the main strategic goal of al Qaeda was not just further terrorist attacks but to achieve the "extinction of America."[24] Al Qaeda is known for long-term planning and for choosing significant historical anniversaries for simultaneous attacks to achieve maximum publicity. It is likely that future attacks will occur on key dates such as August 6, the day when the United States attacked Hiroshima in 1945. Al Qaeda's prime targets include New York, Washington DC, Philadelphia, Chicago, and Los Angeles. According to al Qaeda defectors, one criterion for choosing a target is that the city have a large Jewish population.[25]

The weapons capabilities of radical Islamists go far beyond nuclear weaponry, as we have already established. U.S. Secretary of Defense Donald Rumsfeld released a memorandum titled "The Growing Threat of Cruise Missiles," which warned of the existence of approximately seventy thousand cruise missiles in the military stores of up to eighty nations. Many of these countries are not reliable allies of the West. Further, intelligence reports confirm that as early as 1999 al Qaeda had acquired a significant number of unexploded U.S. cruise missiles that were reengineered to produce usable missiles that could be launched from ships and other platforms.[26]

Weapons of mass destruction would be of less concern if al Qaeda lacked the strategists and the technological sophistication to make effective use of such weapons. But information about the terrorist network's communications capabilities indicates that bin Laden and his followers could make chillingly effective use of the chemical, biological, and nuclear weapons at their disposal. The detonation of nuclear weapons in American cities would profoundly shake the political, social, economic, and military assumptions of the United States. The U.S. response to 9/11 is nothing compared to the magnitude of America's military response to a future terrorist, nuclear attack.

A nuclear attack on New York City could temporarily paralyze the financial center of the nation. Such an attack would devastate tens of thousands of key personnel as well as vital fiber optic and wire networks that link America's capital markets to the rest of the world. The financial center of London and similar districts in Europe, Singapore, and Tokyo are equally vulnerable. Despite billions of dollars being spent to defend these vital communications networks and the massive off-site backup systems, our infinitely complex financial and communication systems remain quite vulnerable to attack.

## ADVANCED TECHNOLOGY FOR SECRET COMMUNICATIONS

Since September 11, 2001, law-enforcement and intelligence agencies throughout the world have attempted to break the encryption techniques used by terrorist networks to relay messages and to implement their plans. *USA Today* cited U.S. and foreign officials who reported that bin Laden and others were using sports chat rooms, pornographic bulletin boards, and other Web sites to hide "maps and photographs of terrorist targets" and to post "instructions for terrorist activities."[27]

A sophisticated computer-espionage communication technique known as steganography is based on the ancient art of embedding a secret message within another, openly available message. Terror groups use a computer technology that prevents intelligence agencies from discovering the hidden messages embedded within a seemingly innocent photograph posted on the Internet. While traditional encryption techniques attempt to create an unbreakable code relying on ciphers to scramble a particular message, steganography has a distinguished and devious history of misleading enemies about the very existence of secret messages that are hidden in plain sight.

Herodotus, the Greek historian who lived centuries before Jesus Christ, described the Greek technique of disguising a secret communication that warned of a coming invasion. The message was written on the bottom interior slot of a wooden tray that held a clay tablet containing the official message. Today, terrorists use steganography that relies on software such as S-Tools, White Noise Storm, MP3 Stego, and Steghide. These computer programs allow users to embed secret messages within computerized digital information—including audio, video, or photographic image files that are transmitted across the Internet.

The computer program Steghide embeds a digital message within .bmp, .wav, and .au computer files, while MP3 Stego hides messages within MP3 files. An especially devious computer program known as Snow embeds messages within additional white space added to the end of every line in a text file or in the body of an e-mail message. Another steganography program, Spam Mimic, encodes a hidden message into what appears to be an easily ignored spam e-mail.

The FBI is concerned that al Qaeda and other terrorist groups may be sending messages to cells in America and Europe by embedding instructions within the video transmissions used by bin Laden. This explains why the White House requests Western television networks to refrain from re-broadcasting bin Laden's messages, in case they might contain hidden stega-nographic information.

It is extremely difficult to find and decode such messages among the billions of audio and photo files that are transmitted across the Internet each month. It is similar to looking for a needle in a haystack, but where the needle has been hidden inside a single straw. While the U.S. National Security Agency's massive supercomputers can decode a message if they know which file it is hidden in, they cannot search every file that travels over the Internet.

## A DANGEROUS MAP OF U.S. INFRASTRUCTURE

In our interconnected world with staggering amounts of uncensored data readily available on the Internet, an enterprising graduate student at George Mason University used his laptop to access little-known Web sites to acquire an enormous amount of sensitive information on key businesses, indus-tries, and organizations critical to the functioning of the U.S. economic infrastructure.

As part of the research for his PhD dissertation, Sean Gorman deter-mined and mapped the most critical fiber-optic information links between cities, financial institutions, industries, government offices, and military bases. Gorman admits he imagined himself in the place of a terrorist. He tried to think as a terrorist might, to determine what information he would need in order to cause the greatest possible damage through his theoretical attacks. Using the map he developed, Gorman could click on a federal reserve bank in Atlanta and its sister institution in Chicago and instantly see the main information links between the two.[28]

According to an article in the *Washington Post* and a September 2003 article in *NewsMax* magazine, major corporations want to acquire Gor-man's doctoral research to learn how to protect themselves against sabotage.

Government security agencies want to classify Gorman's work as top secret, and al Qaeda planners could find it a treasure trove of useful data. As one intelligence analyst commented, Gorman should have immediately received his PhD, and his research should have been classified top secret.[29]

## THE INTERNET AS A TERRORIST RESEARCH TOOL

It's clear that the World Wide Web provides an unparalleled tool for terrorists to use for secret communications, training, and tactical support to link independent cells around the globe. Although intelligence agencies can break the sophisticated encryption codes in use by many terror groups, it takes longer and longer to penetrate their communications. The Internet is home to hundreds of public terrorist chat rooms and technical libraries that provide bomb-making instructions and directions on how to produce various poisons from easily available materials. A staggering number of training manuals are available on terrorist Web sites, including how to get false identification papers, how to safely cross national borders, and how to travel safely through Syria into Iraq. One fascinating fifteen-page Arabic Web document titled "Biological Weapons" supplies instructions on how to find the most effective targets for attack and how to achieve the greatest number of civilian casualties.

Many Western intelligence agencies, including Israel's Mossad, believe al Qaeda has morphed into a global jihad movement that has no central leadership or hierarchal structure. The anonymous and efficient communication made possible by the Internet has allowed the creation of a global alliance of extremists who often choose their own targets. They might choose to cooperate with one particular group for a single mission and then never meet again. This structure makes it difficult for intelligence agencies to penetrate Islamic terrorist groups.[30] In fact, many young Islamic extremists have joined the global jihad without having been directly recruited by al Qaeda cell members.

Terrorist attacks will continue, and a primary target is the nation of Israel. What do these developments mean for the Jewish state and the Western nations that support it? These are questions we will explore in the next section.

# PART III

---

# THE DEEPER SIGNIFICANCE OF GLOBAL TERROR

## *Extreme Islam's Declaration of War Is Foretold in Prophecy*

Having looked at the history, strategy, armaments, and goals of fundamentalist Islam, we now turn to extreme Islam's declaration of war against all enemies. As we look at the escalating conflict between militant Muslims and the State of Israel, we will see that the war actually extends much further, with pledges of violence pronounced against *all* perceived enemies of Islam. Targets include not only Jews but also Christians, Hindus, Buddhists, the West, and even moderate Muslim nations.

Throughout her history, Israel has been invaded, occupied, and carried into exile. With extreme Islam renewing its commitment to rid the world of Jews and the nation of Israel, it is clear that today's acts of terrorism are part of a much larger plan—a literal war that extends far beyond the Middle East. This war of global terror is fueled by a commitment to bring down not just Israel but the entire Western way of life.

# ISLAM'S WAR AGAINST ALL PERCEIVED ENEMIES

## *The Militant Justification for Violence Against Non-Muslims*

Since biblical times, Jews have been targeted repeatedly for oppression and even destruction. In 1948, when the modern State of Israel was created, many people believed that Jews finally could live at peace in their own land. But that dream has proven to be elusive.

As we have seen in the previous chapters, from its birth Islam has used violence to subdue its perceived enemies. And heading the list of enemies are Jews and the State of Israel. Osama bin Laden and al Qaeda have made it clear that the destruction of Israel is a primary goal. The acts of terrorism that headline every day's news are not isolated incidents of deadly religious fanaticism; they are the initial volleys in an all-out war against Israel and the West.

### ISLAMIST PLANS TO DESTROY THE JEWS

The deputy director of the Palestinian Clerics Association, Sheikh Muhammad Ali, declared during a 2005 interview with Hezbollah's Al-Manar TV that jihad was the duty of every Muslim. He added that the coming conquest of all of Palestine would be accomplished through holy war, not through peaceful negotiation.

During a Lebanese Broadcasting Corporation television interview, Syrian defense minister Mustafa Talas declared, "I want to stand in one place and kill the Jew standing before me. If every Arab kills a Jew, there won't be any Jews left at all. We will fight like the Hizballah fights against them in South Lebanon. From the Golan Front, of course—from any front where [the Jews] are situated."[1]

Given the violent nature of such pronouncements, many have wondered why moderate Muslims are reluctant to condemn al Qaeda and other terrorist organizations. Dr. Shaker al-Nabulsi, a Jordanian intellectual living in the United States, considered why respected Islamic religious scholars have not issued a fatwa (religious decree) against terrorism. Al-Nabulsi observed:

> Doesn't the fact that to date not a single fatwa has been issued
> calling for killing bin Laden and the other Al-Qaeda
> leaders…prove that many of the legal scholars who claim to be
> opposed to the waves of terrorism actually embrace these terrorist
> operations and secretly welcome them?[2]

## AN ETHICAL MUSLIM REACTION
## TO SUICIDE TERRORISM AGAINST CIVILIANS

After years of silence from major Islamic organizations regarding terrorist attacks on innocent civilians, four deadly suicide attacks in London on July 7, 2005, provoked certain Islamic authorities to issue a public condemnation. For the first time, Muslim authorities in Canada and the United Kingdom issued an official religious decree that condemned suicide bombing attacks against civilian targets. The British Muslim Forum, a group of respected Muslim scholars, declared: "There is neither place nor justification in Islam for extremism, fanaticism or terrorism. Suicide bombings…are HARAAM, vehemently prohibited in Islam and those who committed these barbaric acts in London are criminals, not martyrs."[3]

An argument over the suicide-bombing tactics arose between a senior al Qaeda leader, Abu Muhammad al-Maqdisi, who is in jail in Jordan, and his protégé, the late Abu Musab al-Zarqawi, a Jordanian who was the operational head of al Qaeda in Iraq and who was killed by U.S. forces on June 7, 2006. On July 2, 2005, al-Maqdisi voiced his criticism of suicide-bombing attacks against civilians and Muslims during several interviews with Arab media. He objected to "the extensive use of suicide operations" carried out by al-Zarqawi's terrorists, in which Muslim civilians were being slaughtered. He stated that suicide operations were not a traditional Islamic means of warfare but were to be resorted to only during exceptional circumstances. Al-Maqdisi also condemned the extensive killing of Shi'ite Muslims in Iraq. He opposed Sunni Muslim declarations that Iraqi Shi'ites were non-Muslims, which allowed them to become targets of violence.

In response, al-Zarqawi rejected the statements of his teacher and declared that Allah ordered the slaughter of all infidels by every means available, even if this inadvertently caused the death of infidels who were not targets, such as women and children, or even the killing of fellow Muslims. In a July 2005 audiotape, al-Zarqawi declared that it was a religious duty to wage jihad against the Shi'ite Muslims because they were actually apostates who formed alliances with the Western crusaders against the Iraqi jihad fighters.[4]

## JIHAD AS TAUGHT IN THE KORAN

Even a cursory reading of the Koran reveals ample grounds for waging holy war against the enemies of Islam if the reader understands jihad to mean violent action against infidels. Here are some of the verses that issue a call to arms:

And fight for the religion of GOD against those who fight against you; but transgress not by attacking them first, for GOD loveth not the transgressors.

And kill them wherever ye find them, and turn them out of that whereof they have dispossessed you; for temptation to idolatry is more grievous than slaughter; yet fight not against them in the holy temple, until they attack you therein; but if they attack you, slay them there. This shall be the reward of infidels. (Sura 2:190–91)

But the recompense of those who fight against GOD and his apostle, and study to act corruptly in the earth, shall be, that they shall be slain, or crucified, or have their hands and their feet cut off on the opposite sides, or be banished [from] the land. This shall be their disgrace in this world, and in the next world they shall suffer a grievous punishment. (Sura 5:33)

When ye encounter the unbelievers, strike off their heads, until ye have made a great slaughter among them; and bind them in bonds; and either give them a free dismission afterwards, or exact a ransom; until the war shall have laid down its arms. This shall ye do. Verily if GOD pleased he could take vengeance on them, without your assistance; but he commandeth you to fight his battles, that he may prove the one of you by the other. And as to those who fight in defence of GOD's true religion, God will not suffer their works to perish. (Sura 47:4)

Therefore fight against them until there be no opposition in favor of idolatry, and the religion be wholly GOD's. (Sura 8:39)

Fight against them who believe not in GOD, nor the last day, and forbid not that which GOD and his apostle have forbidden, and profess not the true religion, of those unto whom the scriptures have been delivered, until they pay tribute by right of subjection, and they be reduced low. (Sura 9:29)

I will cast a dread into the hearts of the unbelievers. Therefore strike off their heads, and strike off all the ends of their fingers. This shall they suffer, because they have resisted GOD and his apostle. (Sura 8:12–13)

## The Koran's Instructions for War

In addition, the Koran provides instructions on making preparations for war against the enemies of Islam, what is to be done in the way of attack, and even how to manage the spoils of war:

Therefore prepare against them what force ye are able, and troops of horse, whereby ye may strike a terror into the enemy of GOD, and your enemy. (Sura 8:60)

If thou take them in war, disperse, by making them an example, those who shall come after them, that they may be warned. (Sura 8:57)

It hath not been granted unto any prophet, that he should possess captives, until he hath made a great slaughter of the infidels in the earth. (Sura 8:67)

How little will ye be warned!

How many cities have we destroyed; which our vengeance overtook by night, or while they were reposing themselves at noon-day!

And their supplication, when our punishment came upon them... (Sura 7:3–5)

And he hath caused such of those who have received the scriptures, as assisted the confederates, to come down out of their
fortresses, and he cast into their hearts terror and dismay: a
part of them ye slew, and a part ye made captives; and God
hath caused you to inherit their land, and their houses, and
their wealth, and a land on which ye have not trodden. (Sura
33:26–27)

Verily if the hypocrites, and those in whose hearts is an infirmity,
and they who raise disturbances in Medina, do not desist, we will
surely stir thee up against them, to chastise them: henceforth they
shall not be suffered to dwell near thee therein, except for a little
time, and being accursed; wherever they are found they shall be
taken, and killed with a general slaughter. (Sura 33:60–61)

To appreciate today's clash of civilizations, it's necessary to understand
a fundamental principle of Islam: any territory that was ever under Islamic
rule can never be surrendered to non-Muslims. Sheikh Muhammad Ali,
deputy director of the Palestinian Clerics Association, has declared that any
land that was ruled by Islam in the past must be liberated by force and
restored to Islamic rule. Further, Ali has stated that the non-Muslim inhabitants of the land are to be subjected to Muslim rule. According to Ali,
"Any land…over which flies the banner of 'There is no god but Allah, and
Muhammad is His Messenger,' and which at a certain point belonged to
the Muslims…it is the duty of all Muslims to do what they can to liberate
this land, wherever it may be."[5]

Islamists believe that they are destined by the Koran and Allah to conquer the entire world. Historically, Muslims have seen the forces of Christianity and Judaism as the only major barriers preventing them from
achieving the goal of global, totalitarian, Islamic government.

This fundamental principle of Islam commits the Muslim world to
unceasing war with all other religions and non-Muslim forces. Even when

Islam finds itself overwhelmed by superior power, as has occurred since the end of the Second Great Jihad, Islam bides its time waiting in "truce" until it regains enough strength to defeat its enemies. Thus, the concept of peace—in the sense of neighboring countries that recognize each other's national sovereignty, honor borders, and respect differences in political systems—is totally foreign to Islam. True peace for Islamic believers can only exist between Muslims and other Muslims, never between Muslims and non-Muslims.

If you understand this, it will help you to understand the Palestinian negotiating position with regard to Israel. In the past, the Palestinian Authority was willing to promise just about anything to achieve a truce with the militarily superior Israeli Defense Forces. At the same time, such a truce was meaningless whenever the opportunity arose for Palestinians to launch an unprovoked terrorist attack against Israeli civilians. For Islam, true peace can be achieved only when Muslims conquer the entire world. Then, and only then, the whole world will become Dar ul-Islam, "the house of peace."

Following peace negotiations in Norway and Washington DC, the Israeli government of Prime Minister Yitzhak Rabin signed the Oslo Agreement on September 13, 1993, with Yasser Arafat, then head of the Palestine Liberation Organization (PLO). The agreement offered greatly weakened Palestinian terrorists the right to return safely from Tunisia to the West Bank and Gaza, along with limited autonomy and the removal of Israeli military control from Jericho and other Palestinian areas. Later, Arafat responded to Arab critics who chastised him for entering into peace negotiations with the hated Jewish enemy. At a Johannesburg, South Africa, mosque, Arafat explained the secret meaning of his "peace" agreement in a speech that was ignored by Western media. Arafat said, "Do you think I signed something with the Jews which is contrary to the rules of Islam?... That's not so. I'm doing exactly what the prophet Mohammed did."[6]

The PLO chairman was referring to the time the prophet Muhammad signed a ten-year peace treaty, the Al-Hudaybiya Treaty, with the Koreish tribe. However, two years later, after Muhammad had trained a ten-thousand-man army, his troops marched on the holy city of Mecca and attacked the Koreish without warning. This victory through treachery became a respected precedent in Islam's early history. By referring to his recently signed peace treaty with Israel as similar to Muhammad's violated treaty with the Koreish, Arafat was telling his listeners that they should not be concerned that the PLO was negotiating true peace with the Jews. It was only a temporary truce that would be violated as soon as military conditions favored the Palestinians.

I have discussed this concept with senior Israeli military and intelligence officials to try to understand Israel's negotiating position with the Palestinians in light of the Islamic commitment to unending warfare and the annihilation of the Jewish people. When I raise this question, usually I am met with evasions. I have concluded that nonreligious Israelis who lack confidence in God's commitment to deliver Israel from her enemies simply ignore the heavy implications of the implacable Islamic hatred of Israel, because there is no realistic prospect of changing the underlying Muslim attitudes that are being taught in mosques throughout the world.

## MUSLIM IMMIGRATION TO THE WEST

Muslim extremists cling to the goal of establishing a totalitarian, global, Islamic government, and one strategy to help bring that about is to replace moderate Islamic governments with governments dedicated to the destruction of all Western influence. A second strategy is to establish a significant Muslim immigrant population in liberal Western democracies. The goal is to have enough Muslim inhabitants to influence European and North American governments against attacking Islamic terrorism. The rioting by Islamic Arab and African youth in France in 2005 produced a wave of politicians arguing for appeasement of the violent offenders and a need to "understand" the social causes of their anger rather than to vigorously respond with police and military force to suppress the rioting.

It is difficult to determine the extent of Islamic immigration to the West because virtually all democracies refuse to collect immigration data that enumerate immigrants according to religious affiliation. Mass Islamic immigration to Europe from Africa, Asia, and the Middle East was produced inadvertently by Western European guest-worker programs from the 1950s through the 1980s. Liberal politicians and sympathetic immigration judges allowed foreign Muslim temporary workers, who were supposed to remain for only a few years on work visas, to take up permanent immigrant status. Family reunification programs created a wave of millions of Muslim immigrants, now joined by tens of millions of descendants. Muslims now form the clear majority of immigrants in Belgium, France, Germany, the Netherlands, and the United Kingdom. It is likely that approximately twenty million Muslims live in Europe, comprising up to 5 percent of the total population.[7]

According to research compiled by Daniel Pipes and Khalid Durn in August 2002, it appears that between two million and three million people in America follow the Muslim faith, making up less than 1 percent of the total population.[8]

## THE WORLDWIDE GROWTH OF CHRISTIANITY OUTSTRIPS THAT OF ISLAM

Muslim populations increase through immigration and through biological growth, but it is erroneous to say that Islam is the world's fastest-growing religion. An article in the 1983 *Reader's Digest Almanac and Yearbook* suggested that the growth rate of Islam worldwide was 235 percent over the previous fifty years, compared with only 47 percent for Christianity, based on the demographic growth rate of the relative religious populations. Unfortunately, most who quote these figures neglect to note that the 235 percent growth rate asserted for Islam is not an annual growth rate but a cumulative growth rate over fifty years. Accurate population statistics accumulated over the last century reveal a remarkable portrait of the astonishing growth of Christianity, which is growing at an accelerated rate today in nations throughout the world.

While Muslim spokesmen and Western media outlets continue to claim that Islam is the world's fastest-growing religion, objective statistical data reveal that the truth is quite different. The annual growth rate of evangelical Christianity is now 4.7 percent, almost twice as great as the current annual growth rate of the Islamic faith (2.6 percent).[9] The same study revealed there were approximately 1.3 billion Muslims in the world as of 2001, compared to an estimated 2.2 billion Christians.

Islam is rapidly expanding in the third world, primarily through biological growth. However, studies reveal that Christianity, and especially evangelical Christianity, is growing even more rapidly in these same nations. Evangelical Christianity is expanding more than three times as quickly as the world population. Christianity is the only religion achieving significant growth through conversion, at a rate almost double that of Islam, according to the most detailed study of world religious growth.[10] The combination of the biological growth of the Christian population in the third world and the unprecedented growth through personal evangelism efforts has resulted in a growth rate never before witnessed in the history of Christianity.

The Lausanne Statistics Task Force examined the growth of evangelical Christianity since the beginning of World War II. Researchers concluded that the growth of the church throughout the globe was far greater than previously reported. Between 1980 and 1997 the number of born-again Christians grew *three times* faster than the world's population:

- In 1940, one person in thirty-two worldwide was a Christian.
- In 1970, one person in nineteen worldwide was a Christian.
- In 1980, one person in sixteen worldwide was a Christian.
- In 1997, one person in ten worldwide was a Christian.[11]

Since the end of World War II, the number of Christians throughout the world has grown by an astonishing 1,300 percent while the world's population has grown by only 400 percent. It is important to note that this explosive growth is taking place almost entirely within the evangelical and charismatic segments of the church. Evangelical Christianity worldwide in only six decades has grown from 40 million believers in 1934 to more than 540 million in 2001.

Christianity began two thousand years ago in Israel and rapidly spread throughout the Middle East and west into North Africa, Ethiopia, and Sudan. It spread east into Saudi Arabia, Persia, and India, and north into Asia, including Armenia. The apostle Paul and numerous other early apostles and missionaries took the gospel to the farthest reaches of the Roman Empire. The faith spread in Europe, then to Great Britain and Ireland, and finally north to the Scandinavian countries and Russia. During the first few centuries of the church, the center of Christianity was western Europe and the Middle East, with branches beginning to penetrate eastward to Persia and south to Ethiopia. In the former Eastern Roman Empire, the Byzantine Church became a centralizing force to organize society in the eastern Middle East (Turkey, Syria, Israel, and Egypt).

In the centuries after the Protestant Reformation in the early 1500s, thousands of missionaries launched evangelizing efforts throughout Europe and North America. Eventually millions of new Christians began to share their faith with others and supported missionaries who took their faith in Jesus to the third world. Over the centuries, the center of gravity of Christianity began to shift from Europe to North America. Finally, as millions of people in the third world accepted Christ as their Savior and became missionaries themselves, hundreds of millions in Africa, South America, and Asia adopted the Christian faith and began to effectively share their new faith with those of their own nationalities.

After a century of dedicated efforts by Western missionaries, perhaps as many as a million Chinese had accepted Jesus Christ. However, after foreign missionaries were expelled from China in 1949 during the Communist Revolution, the million Chinese Christians began to share their faith with other Chinese citizens. Despite staggering martyrdom and persecution, the underground church in China exploded to 120 million dedicated believers. A similar situation occurred in Africa after a century of slow penetration of the faith that achieved approximately 2 million evangelical or charismatic Christian believers by 1900. A century later, studies suggest that there are 200 million evangelical or charismatic followers of Christ living in Africa. In that same century in South America, the born-again population rose from 1 million believers to 170 million evangelical followers of Christ. In each country there obviously were millions of additional followers of Christ who were members of the Roman Catholic Church and other mainline denominations.[12]

While many have the impression that Islam is taking over national populations through immigration, biological growth, and religious conversion, the most reliable statistics don't support that conclusion. The church is growing at a more rapid pace, and the growth of Christianity through conversion is far greater than that of Islam.

The mere existence of Christians and Jews anywhere in the world is a threat to extremist Muslims. In the next chapter we will examine evidence that links Saddam Hussein and Iraqi intelligence with Osama bin Laden and the terrorist attacks of the al Qaeda network.

# 9

# IRAQ'S TERROR CONNECTION

*Evidence of Saddam Hussein's Support of al Qaeda*

The debate continues over whether Saddam Hussein supported terrorism and whether Iraq possessed WMD prior to the 2003 invasion by coalition forces. The Bush administration pointed to Iraq's backing of terrorism as one reason Hussein's regime needed to be removed from power. However, liberal groups and much of the major news media have denied there is substantial evidence to back up this claim.

Following the March 2003 invasion of Iraq, coalition forces shut down three major terrorist training camps. The largest training base was Salman Pak, approximately fifteen miles southeast of Baghdad. Numerous Iraqi defectors have confirmed that the camp possessed a Boeing passenger jet on which terrorists practiced hijacking and air-piracy skills. Salman Pak also included an urban-assault training site and a three-car train for simulating attacks on railways. This site operated with the funding and supervision of Hussein's intelligence service.[1]

A former Iraqi army captain, Sabah Khodada, worked at Salman Pak before the 2003 war. Khodada gave an interview to the PBS television program *Frontline* on October 14, 2001. He admitted, "This camp is specialized in exporting terrorism to the whole world.... Training includes hijacking...of airplanes, trains, public buses, and planting explosives in cities...how to prepare for suicidal operations.... We saw people getting trained to hijack airplanes.... They are even trained how to use utensils for food [as weapons], like forks and knives provided in the plane."[2]

Despite the many denials by critics of the Bush administration, there is overwhelming evidence that Hussein and Iraqi intelligence agencies provided vast amounts of money, diplomatic courier services, shelter, medical care, and training to terrorists from various Islamic terror groups, including al Qaeda. It is known, for example, that Iraq assisted the terrorists responsible for the 1993 World Trade Center bombing. There also is evidence that links Iraq to the 2001 attacks on the Pentagon and the World Trade Center.

Muhammad Atta was found to be the lead hijacker in the plot to crash commercial airliners into strategic U.S. targets on September 11, 2001. Atta organized the four hijacking teams and was the pilot on one of the jets that struck the World Trade Center.

Hynek Kmonicek, the Czech Republic's U.N. ambassador, confirmed that contact was made between Atta and an Iraqi intelligence agent. In a letter written to attorney James Beasley Jr., who filed a wrongful-death lawsuit against Hussein after the 9/11 World Trade Center attack, Kmonicek stated: "In this moment we can confirm, that during the next stay of Mr. Muhammad Atta in the Czech Republic, there was the contact with the official of the Iraqi intelligence, Mr. Al Ani, Ahmed Khalin Ibrahim Samir."[3]

And there is more. According to Iraq's coalition government, Muhammad Atta was trained in Baghdad by Palestinian terrorist Abu Nidal. The *Toronto National Post* reported in December 2003 the discovery of a secret memo to Saddam Hussein that gives details of a visit by Atta to the Iraqi capital just weeks before the 9/11 attacks.[4]

The memo, obtained exclusively by the *National Post,* was written by Tahir Jalil Habbush al-Tikriti, the former head of the Iraqi Intelligence

Service and cousin to Saddam Hussein. Dated July 1, 2001, it outlines a three-day "work program" for Atta at Abu Nidal's base in Baghdad, the *Telegraph* said. (Nidal, headquartered in Baghdad for more than fifteen years, was the leading Palestinian terrorist who used hijacking as a form of terrorism in the 1970s and 1980s. He was responsible for the failed 1982 assassination attempt on the Israeli ambassador to the United Kingdom.[5]) Habbush, according to the memo, says Atta "displayed extraordinary effort" and demonstrated his ability to lead the team that would be "responsible for attacking the targets that we have agreed to destroy," the *Telegraph* reported.[6] Allawi, the interim president of Iraq, insisted the document was genuine, although Iraqi officials refused to disclose how they obtained it.

## THE 9/11 COMMISSION MISSED LINKS
## BETWEEN BIN LADEN AND HUSSEIN

While the 9/11 Commission wrote that there was "no credible evidence" of cooperation between Iraq and al Qaeda concerning the September 11 attacks, the commission overlooked more than ten years of connections and cooperation between Hussein's regime and bin Laden's terrorist network.

An article published in Baghdad on January 14, 2002, entitled "Iraqis Vote Osama bin Laden Man of 2001," confirmed both Hussein's and the Iraqi population's support for 9/11. According to an Iraqi radio and television survey, 93 percent of Iraqis voted for bin Laden as the top political personality of Iraq for 2001. The article, posted online by the *Namibian,* quoted the survey's declaration: "The Saudi dissident Osama bin Laden is the political personality of 2001 for his hostility towards American hegemony and aggression against Afghanistan." According to the article, the official Iraqi daily newspaper, *Al-Jumhuriya,* and the weekly newspaper *Al-Zawra* also elected bin Laden as the man of the year in honor of his devastating terrorist attack on American civilians.[7]

The 9/11 Commission acknowledged that bin Laden made overtures to Hussein while bin Laden was in Sudan in the mid-1990s and again after he went to Afghanistan in 1996. But the commission concluded that these contacts "do not appear to have resulted in a collaborative relationship." The report also seemed to rely heavily on the word of two of bin Laden's most senior associates who, during interrogations, "adamantly denied that any ties existed between al-Qaida and Iraq." Of course, such assertions may be self-serving.[8]

President George W. Bush, who publicly minimized the bin Laden–Iraq connection as a pretext for the invasion of Iraq, quickly responded to the 9/11 Commission's report by affirming that "numerous contacts" between Iraq and al Qaeda did indeed justify the U.S.-led invasion. "There was a relationship between Iraq and Saddam and al-Qaeda," Bush told reporters. "This administration never said that the 9/11 attacks were orchestrated between Saddam and al-Qaeda. We did say there were numerous contacts between Saddam and al-Qaeda."[9]

Yossef Bodansky, author of *Bin Laden: The Man Who Declared War on America,* which was published before the 9/11 attacks, documents numerous contacts and meetings between bin Laden's agents and agents of Saddam Hussein. In addition, Bodansky, Congress's highest-level terrorism advisor, declared that the relationship between Iraq and al Qaeda predated the September 11 attacks by a decade and continued thereafter.[10] Almost one hundred CIA reports of Iraqi–al Qaeda cooperation extend back to 1992, according to WorldNetDaily sources.

Shortly before the 9/11 attacks, a group of al Qaeda fighters left Afghanistan and set up terrorist camps in Iraq as a backup base. Bin Laden's jihadists established such a base in the town of Al Biyara as well as nearby mountain villages, where some Kurdish extremists had begun imposing strict Islamic rule, much like Afghanistan's former Taliban regime.[11] Ansar al-Islam, the terrorist group in northern Iraq, is led by an Iraqi Kurd named Nejmeddin Faraj Ahmad (also known as Mullah Krekar), who trained with bin Laden in Afghanistan in the 1980s.[12] On January 27, 2004, White House spokesman Ari Fleischer reported that terrorist detainees from

Afghanistan had implicated Iraq in providing training and support to al Qaeda.[13]

Perhaps more interesting is the contention of terrorism expert Laurie Mylroie, author of *The War Against America*. She claims that senior al Qaeda operative Khalid Sheikh Muhammad, captured in Pakistan, is actually an Iraqi intelligence agent, a fact that would serve as direct, smoking-gun evidence linking Saddam Hussein to the terror attack on America in 2001. Mylroie, an adjunct fellow at the American Enterprise Institute, explains that Khalid Sheikh Muhammad was captured in Rawalpindi, Pakistan, on March 1, 2003, and has been providing U.S. interrogators with critical information about al Qaeda operations and future attack plots, according to U.S. officials.[14]

As the operational leader of al Qaeda terrorist networks, Muhammad has been identified as the mastermind of the 9/11 terror attacks. He also is believed to have planned the 1998 simultaneous U.S. embassy bombings in East Africa and the bombing of the USS *Cole* in Yemen in 2000. Mylroie maintains that Muhammad is actually a Pakistani Baluch. (Baluchs are Sunni Muslims who live in the desert regions of eastern Iran and northwestern Pakistan—Baluchistan—and have longstanding ties to Iraqi intelligence.) Another Baluch is Ramzi Yousef, Muhammad's nephew, the mastermind behind the 1993 World Trade Center bombing. The two collaborated with a third Baluch in 1995, Abdul Hakam Murad, another relative, in an unsuccessful plot to simultaneously bomb twelve U.S. airplanes. The plot, called Project Bojinka, also involved ramming a fuel-laden airliner into the Pentagon.[15]

Mylroie said her research revealed that Muhammad, Yousef, and Murad are all part of a tight terrorist circle following orders from al Qaeda.[16] Their identities are based on documents from Kuwaiti files that predate Kuwait's liberation from Iraq's occupation army in 1992. These documents form the basis of Mylroie's false-identity theory regarding Iraqi terrorists. When Iraq occupied Kuwait in 1990 and 1991, it used captured

Kuwaiti files to create false identities for key Iraqi terrorist agents, according to Mylroie.

There is clear evidence that Ramzi Yousef's file was tampered with. The front pages of his passport, including his picture and signature, are missing. Extraneous information was also inserted, including the notation that Yousef and his family left Kuwait on August 26, 1990, during Iraq's occupation of Kuwait, and traveled through Iraq on their way to Pakistani Baluchistan in Iran. Mylroie points out that people don't normally provide authorities with itineraries of their travel plans when crossing a border. She concluded that Yousef is an Iraqi secret intelligence agent who assumed the identity of someone named Abdul Basit Karim, a Kuwaiti who disappeared during Iraq's occupation. Records show Yousef entered the United States on an Iraqi passport in the name of Ramzi Yousef, but he fled using a passport in the name of Abdul Basit Karim.[17] According to Mylroie, the New York office of the FBI—particularly its director, Jim Fox—believed that the 1993 World Trade Center bombing was an Iraqi intelligence operation.

The available evidence strongly suggests that for many years Iraqi intelligence supported not only the goals but also the work of al Qaeda. The war on terror is a costly and prolonged—but absolutely necessary—battle against sworn enemies of Israel and the West. The evidence presents a compelling argument for the necessity of deposing Saddam Hussein.

10

# THE DEEPER THREAT
# OF TERRORISM

*The Terrorists' True Goals and How the Media Get It Wrong*

The global war being waged by Islamic terrorists is not a conventional battle over territory or disputed national borders. It's not a war with troops in uniform and easily identifiable fronts and battle lines. And because it does not conform to the strategies or rules of conventional warfare, it's easy to miss what is really going on. The news media tend to dismiss the idea that militant Islam has declared global war against Western democratic values and the Western way of life.

But those who study the statements and teachings of extreme Islam—not to mention the acts of terrorism—know that suicide bombings, the ongoing insurgency in Iraq, the attacks by remnants of the Taliban in Afghanistan, and violent clashes in Africa, Asia, the Middle East, and Europe are far from isolated flareups of religious tension. Quite the opposite: they are manifestations of an ongoing and coordinated war that has global implications. This war is not limited to certain flash points such as Israel, Iraq, Afghanistan, Indonesia, or Sudan. It's a well-armed and carefully planned battle that will settle for nothing less than the overthrow of all non-Islamic governments and societies around the world.

With the 1979 revolution that toppled the shah of Iran, Ayatollah Ruhollah Khomeini achieved his goal of creating the first revolutionary Islamic state. He established rigid medieval shari'ah law to govern the lives, both civil and religious, of all Iranian citizens. During the quarter century that followed the Iranian revolution, the world witnessed the staggering growth in the number and ferocity of terror attacks against civilian targets. While the vast majority of the world's 1.2 billion Muslims do not support terrorism, a number of studies reveal that hundreds of millions of Muslims sympathize with these acts of terrorism—including suicide attacks on Christians, Jews, moderate Muslims, and other perceived enemies.

According to *Al Hayat al Jadida,* an Arabic newspaper funded by the Palestinian Authority, the Palestinian assessment of the World Trade Center attacks in 2001 was that "the suicide bombers of today are the noble successors of their predecessors. These suicide bombers are the salt of the earth, the engines of history…they are the most honourable among us."[1] Numerous polls have revealed that up to 73 percent of Palestinians expressed support for suicide missions against U.S. interests in the Middle East. According to the Associated Press Television News, the news agency that filmed a demonstration held in the West Bank and Gaza, "On hearing news of the American deaths, thousands of Palestinians in Nablus ran into the street chanting, 'Allah is great.'" But according to a report by Timothy Noah of *Slate* online magazine, the footage was never shown. "The cameraman was told by Arafat's Cabinet secretary that if it was shown, the cameraman's life could not be guaranteed."[2]

## MORAL CONFUSION AND THE GLOBAL WAR AGAINST THE WEST

Amazingly, moral relativism leads many in the West to avoid condemning terrorism for the evil that it is. For example, in the fall of 2002, a number of news articles quoted both Palestinian and al Qaeda sources defending their terrorist attacks against civilians by stating, "One man's terrorist is another man's freedom fighter."[3]

While the desire to avoid identifying militant Islamists as evil terrorists is increasingly common in the media, this reflects widespread ethical confusion. Too many people in the West make the mistake of accepting the moral equivalence between those who use violence against military and other noncivilian targets to achieve political freedom and terrorists who plan violent attacks against innocent civilians and civilian targets. The latter choose nonmilitary targets in order to gain maximum media coverage and political impact.

While military conflict inevitably involves the unintended infliction of violence upon some civilians, that is not the purpose of such attacks. However, those who embrace terrorism as a political strategy purposely target civilians in an attempt to cause the greatest possible terror and emotional distress. Thus they target places of worship, shopping districts, and schools.

In a morally bankrupt attempt to justify terrorist attacks against Jewish civilians, the PLO and Hamas declared that there is no such thing as an "innocent" Israeli civilian. They claim that even Israeli babies and grandparents are legitimate targets because babies will grow up to serve in the Israeli military and all Israeli citizens support the military with taxes.

Such rationalizing might be expected from the Palestinian leadership, but why do the news media fail to make a moral distinction? In spite of the rising tide of terrorism, the Western media have adopted policies that cloud the truth about the global war being waged by militant Islam. Several years ago Reuters began instructing its reporters and editors to eliminate the use of the word *terrorist* to describe Islamic bombers, even if they identified themselves as terrorists.

Chechen terrorists murdered hundreds of innocent children in Breslan, Russia. Nineteen Islamic hijackers slaughtered three thousand office workers, military personnel, and airline passengers on September 11, 2001, in the eastern United States. Four Islamic bombers callously murdered more than fifty London commuters on September 7, 2005. In the first few days following the London bombings, the Canadian Broadcasting Corporation editors and reporters were so horrified that they felt compelled to identify the perpetrators as "terrorists" and referred to the savage attack as a "terrorist attack." But political correctness rapidly reasserted itself, and Tony Burman, CBC's editor in chief, issued instructions to reporters to "exercise extreme caution before using either word."[4]

According to Burman's memo, the words *terrorist* and *terrorism* should be used only if they are part of a direct quote. "We don't judge specific acts as 'terrorism' or people as 'terrorists,' " his memo stated. It is astonishing that its news reports use "neutral language" to describe attacks on citizens because the word *terrorism* is "a highly controversial term that can leave journalists taking sides in a conflict."[5]

How can any moral person not take sides? The refusal to take a moral position that identifies as terrorists those who indiscriminately kill non-combatants reveals a horrifying moral vacuum in the news media. It's no wonder that so many in the West have failed to grasp the truth that a global war between militant Islam and the West is already well under way.

The euphemism now used by most Western media to describe terrorists is *militants.* As an example of the efforts to avoid identifying Islamic killers as terrorists, consider a review of the worldwide press coverage of the horrific Chechen terrorist attack on September 3, 2004, against several hundred schoolchildren and teachers in Breslan, Russia. In an article reviewing coverage of this savage attack, Daniel Pipes, director of the Middle East Forum, listed the following euphemisms that were substituted for the word *terrorists* by various international media organizations:

- National Public Radio: "assailants"
- *Economist:* "attackers"
- *Guardian:* "bombers"
- Agence France-Presse: "commandos"
- *Washington Post:* "fighters"
- *New York Post:* "guerrillas"

- Reuters: "gunmen"
- *Chicago Tribune:* "militants"
- *Pakistan Times:* "activists"[6]

In spite of widespread ethical confusion and news media policies that insist on euphemisms, here is the definition of terrorism as set forth in Federal Statute 22 U.S.C. § 2656f(d):

> The term "terrorism" means premeditated, politically motivated violence perpetrated against non-combatant targets by subnational groups or clandestine agents, usually intended to influence an audience.
>
> The term "international terrorism" means terrorism that involves citizens or targets in the territory of more than one country.
>
> The term "terrorist group" means any group practicing, or that has significant subgroups that practice, international terrorism.

## THE RECRUITING OF AN ISLAMIC TERRORIST

It is not an easy step for someone who grows up in a peaceful society to commit to engage in violent terrorist activities. Intelligence reports indicate that the first step involves using books, comics, and videos to condition recruits to begin imagining life as jihad warriors. In addition, potential recruits are exposed to former jihad warriors in their mosques and communities. These ex-warriors are presented as heroes and positive role models.

It is important that new recruits begin their duties doing nonviolent activities, such as researching or raising money for the al Qaeda cause in Palestine, Chechnya, or Bosnia. Recruits in the West usually begin as sympathizers who are assigned modest duties to test their level of interest and commitment to the cause.

If recruits prove to be highly motivated, they are guided toward a more violent group that provides weekend paramilitary training in surveillance, the use of weapons, and other skills. The next step is usually to travel to Sudan or Pakistan to obtain further weapons and tactics training. Finally, when the trainers deem a recruit is ready, he is exposed to real fighting for a few weeks in one of the open-conflict areas. After the completion of his training, including bomb making and sabotage, a recruit normally meets with a senior al Qaeda leader, possibly Osama bin Laden himself, where he is required to take the oath of allegiance *(bayat)* in which he pledges absolute loyalty and obedience to al Qaeda. The bayat, as created by bin Laden, includes the following wording: "The pledge of God and His covenant is upon me, to listen and obey the superiors, who are doing this work, in energy, early-rising, difficulty, and easiness, and for His superiority upon us, so that the word of God will be the highest, and His religion victorious."[7]

After completing the training and taking the oath, the recruit is assigned a mission to attack either enemies who are not Islamic or a target connected with Muslims who do not adhere to extremist Islamic doctrine.

## THE MOTIVES OF SUICIDE BOMBERS

Most Westerners are puzzled by the motivation of young Arab men (and a few women) who volunteer for suicide-bombing attacks. What could possibly influence them to strap bombs to their bodies, go to prayer, say goodbye to their families, and then move among innocent civilians with the purpose of killing as many men, women, and children as possible? What religious beliefs could lead people to destroy their lives and the lives of dozens of innocent civilians?

The first thing to recognize is that the Muslim religious community does not consider a suicide bomber to have committed suicide. Rather, the bomber is called a *shahid,* a martyr who dies as a hero. Many suicide bombers come from families in the lower socioeconomic class. Once the bomber has completed his mission, his family usually receives honor and a substantial pension, as well as other financial rewards from Arab authorities and his community. These rewards are paid to the families by Saudi Arabia, Hamas, and the Palestinian Authority (and by Iraq before Saddam Hussein's defeat).

The personal motivation of suicide bombers includes the belief that they will receive tremendous pleasures and rewards in the afterlife. Bombers are promised that they will enjoy eternity in paradise with the loving attentions of seventy-two young virgins, who will serve them sexually forever. They also are promised unlimited indulgence in wine, permission to see the face of Allah, and the privilege to give life in paradise to seventy of their chosen relatives and friends. It is interesting to note, however, that many nonfundamentalist Islamic teachers condemn suicide bombings as a violation of the Koran's rules against suicide.

There is no guarantee of paradise for Muslims in the Koran as a result of their belief or good deeds. Muhammad taught that all Muslims would find that their good deeds would be weighed against their evil deeds on the final day of judgment, and only then would they know their eternal destiny in paradise or hell. However, shahids are guaranteed paradise for themselves and seventy chosen loved ones. This helps explain why families and friends usually celebrate a relative's successful suicide bombing.

On June 2, 2001, a suicide bombing at a Tel Aviv discotheque killed twenty young Israelis. The bomber was Saeed Hotary, a twenty-two-year-old Jordanian who lived in the West Bank. He was trained and sent on his deadly mission by the terrorist group Hamas. Saeed's father, Hassan, proudly announced to the Associated Press, "I am very happy and proud of what my son did and I hope all the men of Palestine and Jordan would do the same."[8]

The majority of suicide bombers are between eighteen and twenty-seven years old, unmarried, unemployed, and poor. A significant number have the desire to avenge the death of a relative or associate who has been killed by the Israeli military. It is interesting to note that some terrorists who were trained as shahids admitted they were taken to a graveyard and placed inside a grave for several hours to overcome any fear of death.[9]

An Israeli newspaper published the following profile of the typical suicide bomber, based on interviews with defense officials and with failed
bombers:

- Forty-seven percent of the bombers are educated at the elementary-
  school level, with an additional 29 percent in possession of at least
  a high-school education.
- Eighty-three percent are unmarried.
- Sixty-four percent are aged eighteen to twenty-three, with the
  majority of the remaining bombers being younger than age thirty.
- Sixty-eight percent of the suicide bombers have come from the
  Gaza Strip.[10]

According to a May 2001 poll of Palestinian adults from both the Gaza
Strip and the West Bank (including East Jerusalem), conducted by Dr.
Nabil Kukali and the Palestinian Center for Public Opinion, a "substantial
majority (76.1%) support suicidal attacks like that of Netanya [in May 18,
2001], whereas 12.5% oppose, and 11.4% express no opinion."[11]

The widespread popularity of suicide bombing as a weapon against
Israeli civilians reveals the depth of hatred in the hearts of a large majority
of the Palestinian people. This deeply felt hatred can only be transformed
supernaturally by Jesus Christ when He returns to heal the hearts of both
the Arabs and Jews, reconciling them finally to live as brothers in the
Promised Land and throughout the Middle East.

### Stopping Suicide Bombers

Untold lives would be spared if suicide bombers could be intercepted before
carrying out their missions. Aside from security barriers, the best defense
against suicide bombers is the work of deep-penetration Arab agents who
identify the indicators that a young man is being groomed to carry out a suicide mission.

In addition, Israeli and U.S. security agents are using sophisticated
technologies that detect explosives from a distance. Such detection abilities
give law-enforcement personnel the opportunity to prevent bombings by

stopping would-be attackers before they reach their targets. Once Israeli technology can detect large amounts of explosives at distances of up to a mile, the explosives can be detonated by radio signal or a sniper can be dispatched to shoot the bomber far from his target.

## THE WAR WE MUST WIN

Western democracies are initially reluctant to respond decisively to obvious dangers. However, when they awaken to the seriousness of a threat, democracies prove to be a much more formidable opponent than any totalitarian regime. Democracies that have been attacked eventually rouse themselves to defend their people, territory, and freedoms with a relentlessness that demands nothing less than the enemy's total military destruction.

The world now faces the prospect of a costly, decades-long war to eradicate the threat from Islamic extremists. This unprecedented war will test political resolve, military and intelligence capabilities, and the moral resources of the populations and leadership of the Western nations. We will succeed in defeating both the terrorist-supporting nations and the one-hundred-thousand-plus terrorists who have dedicated themselves to the destruction of Western freedom.

Since the 1979 Islamic Revolution in Iran, a number of nations, led by Saudi Arabia and Iran, have provided massive amounts of weapons, financing, intelligence, training, and shelter for tens of thousands of Islamic terrorists dedicated to the destruction of Israel and the Jewish and Christian population of the Western nations. The nations that actively support terrorism financially and with military training and weapons include Sudan, Yemen, Syria, Iran, Somalia, and Libya. (Recently Libya has shut down its terrorist training camps and has surrendered its WMD program.) Afghanistan and Iraq were the most important training bases and supporters of al Qaeda terrorists until that support was brought to an end by U.S. and allied forces in 2002 and 2003.

As the global coalition against terror continues to destroy support bases and disrupt channels of financial support, terrorists are losing their ability to stage massive attacks. Al Qaeda has been largely unsuccessful in mounting simultaneous terrorist attacks since the March 11, 2004, bombings of the Madrid trains, which killed 191 citizens and wounded another 1,741. Eventually, the scourge of global Islamic terrorism will be reduced to the status of a continuing police problem.

However, because there are millions of soft targets—including hotels, churches, synagogues, shopping malls, and schools—that can't be protected at all times, terrorists will periodically launch successful attacks. Over time, vigilance and aggressive attacks against terror cells will wear down their confidence and numbers to the point that the West will win the war against al Qaeda and its allies.

Christians and others who are familiar with the Old Testament should not be surprised that extreme Islam is waging all-out war against Israel and the West. The global conflict is based on an ancient hatred that dates back to the beginning of the history of the descendants of Abraham. God prophesied there would be an irreconcilable hatred in the heart of Ishmael, the son of the Egyptian Hagar, toward his brother, Isaac, the ancestor of the Jewish people. The history of the last four thousand years has demonstrated this hatred, which culminates today in the bitter dispute between the Palestinians and their Arab brethren against their Jewish brethren, who seek to live in peace with the Arabs in the Promised Land. The last section of the book will examine how God has set the stage for the final resolution of this struggle by the fulfillment of the prophesied events of the last days.

# PART IV

## OUR GENERATION HAS ENTERED THE LAST DAYS

*Clear Signs of the Fulfillment of Biblical Prophecy*

With its declaration of war against Israel and Israel's supporters in the West, extreme Islam is playing a central role in fulfilling the prophesied events of the last days. We now turn to current developments in the war on terror to explore how these events match up with ancient biblical prophecies. Studying prophecy helps explain not only what is happening in our unsettled world but also reveals what will happen in the near future—in our own generation. Ezekiel, Daniel, King David, Isaiah, Zechariah, Jeremiah, the apostle John, Jesus Christ, and other prophets speaking two thousand or more years ago painted a vivid, detailed picture of the events that will lead up to the return to earth of Jesus the Messiah. We are witnessing the opening scenes of this unfolding drama today.

# 11

# THE ARAB WAR
# AGAINST ISRAEL

*Overwhelming Evidence of the Commitment
to Eliminate the Jews from Palestine*

Arab leaders have made no secret of their desire to annihilate the Jewish population of Israel. The day that the modern State of Israel was declared to be a nation, the Secretary General of the Arab League, Azzam Pasha, announced at a press conference in Cairo on May 15, 1948: "This will be a war of extermination and a momentous massacre...like the Mongolian massacres and the Crusades."[1]

In an interview published in the newspaper *Akhbar al-Yom* on October 11, 1947, Pasha reported that there were "three characteristics of the future war: the belief in glorious death as a road to paradise, the opportunities of lust and the Bedouin love of slaughter for its own sake."[2]

Muhammad Saleh ed-Din, Egypt's then minister of foreign affairs, revealed in 1949 the true purpose of the Arab demand that all Arab refugees (and their descendants) be allowed to return and settle in Israel. "Let it therefore be known and appreciated that, in demanding the restoration of the refugees to Palestine, the Arabs intend that they shall return as the masters of the homeland, and not as slaves," he stated. "With a greater clarity, they mean the liquidation of the State of Israel."[3]

The demand that Arab refugees be allowed to settle in Israel stands in stark contrast to provisions that were made for refugees after World War II. Despite the fact that more than forty million people were displaced by the war, no one called for their return to their former lands. The United Nations plan for refugees has always called for their settlement in their new nations so they can begin to rebuild their lives. With Poland, Germany, Vietnam, Cambodia, and dozens of other nations, refugees have been settled in new countries. But in the case of Palestine, the world demanded that common practice and justice be ignored, forcing displaced Arabs to remain in refugee camps for more than a half century. The demand that the refugees and their millions of descendants be returned to the tiny nation of Israel (which is smaller than Rhode Island) is irresponsible. The great majority of these Palestinians were born since 1948 and have never lived in Israel or even seen their ancestors' homes in Israel.

## WHAT ABOUT JEWISH REFUGEES?

In the discussion of the Palestinians, the hardships and struggles faced by Jewish refugees for thousands of years have been overlooked. An equal or greater number of Jews, who lived for thousands of years as exiles in the Arab world and in other regions of the world, were forced to become refugees and flee for their lives. It is estimated that in 1948 more than 850,000 Jews were living in Arab countries. Many of these Jewish refugees and their ancestors had lived there for many generations. (Today there are only a thousand or fewer Jews living in twenty-one Arab nations.)

In 1948, when the State of Israel was founded, Jews living in Arab countries were forced to abandon their possessions, lands, businesses, and money and flee to the only place in the world that would accept them—Israel. Despite the pleasant picture presented by many commentators of thousands of years of Arab-Jewish coexistence prior to Israel's creation, the sad truth is that most Jews living in Arab countries lived in oppression and faced racial hatred akin to that practiced by the Nazis and Russians in the last century. The claims to compensation by the Jewish refugees who fled Arab countries to settle in Israel would far outweigh any similar claims that could legitimately be made by Arab refugees who left Israel in 1948.

## THE MYTH OF THE NATION OF PALESTINE

Despite the fact that Jordan occupied the West Bank and East Jerusalem from 1948 until 1967, no one publicly called for the creation of a State of Palestine. Not one government, nor any Palestinian group, asked to create an official Palestinian homeland. The myth of Palestine had not yet been created.

During the Paris Peace Conference in February 1919, the Muslim chairman of the delegation from Syria declared, "The only Arab domination since the Conquest in AD 635 hardly lasted, as such, 22 years."[4]

Historian Bernard Lewis wrote, "From the end of the Jewish state in antiquity [AD 70] to the beginning of British rule [AD 1918], the area now designated by the name Palestine was not a country and had no frontier, only administrative boundaries; it was a group of provincial subdivisions, by no means always the same, within a larger entity."[5]

There has never been an Arab state in Palestine in all of recorded history. This ancient land was a Jewish nation from the conquest by Joshua in 1451 BC until the defeat of the Jewish nation by the legions of Rome in AD 70. During thousands of years of persecution and exile, the Jews have always prayed to return to their beloved Jerusalem. A constant refrain of a traditional Hebrew prayer is "Next year in Jerusalem."

Despite enormous persecution over the centuries, thousands of Jews remained in the land. Many of the current Sephardic Jews can trace their families back thirteen or more generations. The Arabs living in Palestine never created an independent political unit or a self-governing state. As recorded in the Palestine Royal Commission Report: "In the twelve centuries or more that have passed since the Arab conquest, Palestine has virtually dropped out of history."[6] The claim that the Palestinians have been there "from time immemorial" is simply a fiction.

The Palestinians claim that the only place they could possibly establish a Palestinian state must be in a small area of the West Bank, Gaza, and Israel. However, vast areas of Arab-controlled land are available. The Arab nations could easily provide sufficient land and oil revenues to create a prosperous Palestinian state. That they choose not to do so is evidence of a lack of true concern on the part of the Arab nations.

|  | Land area in square miles | Population |
|---|---|---|
| Islamic Nations | 8,879,548 | 804,500,000 |
| United States | 3,540,939 | 252,000,000 |
| Israel | 8,000 | 6,000,000 |

The total land area of the thirty-five Islamic nations is more than 1,109 times larger than Israel's. When the media suggest that the only place the Palestinians could possibly settle is in Israel, they are ignoring the fact that the Islamic and Arab countries possess vast undeveloped areas and own enormous oil reserves that could easily provide the basis for rebuilding productive lives for the Palestinian people who share their culture, language, and religion.

## THE LONG-TERM ARAB PLAN TO DESTROY ISRAEL

The Arab commitment to eliminate the Jews was reaffirmed throughout the twentieth century. In 1940, the Mufti of Jerusalem, the supreme Muslim Arab authority in Palestine, requested that Nazi Germany and Italy allow the Arabs "to settle the question of Jewish elements in Palestine and other Arab countries in accordance with the national and racial interests of the Arabs and along lines similar to those used to solve the Jewish question in Germany and Italy."[7]

That blatant pronouncement during World War II was no aberration. For evidence of the ongoing Arab plan to destroy Israel, you need look no further than the Palestine Liberation Organization (PLO). Since its creation in 1967, the PLO has dedicated itself to the total destruction of the State of Israel, including its Jewish population. In fact, during the last several years while the PLO and the Palestinian Authority have given assurances that they are renouncing terrorism, they have launched thousands of separate terrorist acts against Jews in Israel.

After suffering defeat in 1967 in the Six-Day War, the Arab leadership began to reconsider how best to destroy Israel. They decided that open discussion about "throwing Israel into the sea" and "turning the Mediterranean red with Jewish blood" was not playing well in the Western media, so Arab leaders decided to downplay the bellicose rhetoric and turn instead to discussing the need to create a Palestinian homeland. This ministate in the bosom of Israel would make Israel virtually indefensible militarily because the Jewish state would be less than ten miles wide at the narrowest part of the country. A powerful Arab armored force could invade and cut the tiny State of Israel in two within a few hours.

Arab leaders have stated on Arabic radio that the demand for a Palestine homeland is simply the first stage of a multistage plan to make Israel militarily indefensible. The later stages will involve a buildup of forces around the tiny state and then, finally, an invasion force large enough to wipe out the Jewish population.

### The PLO "Phased Plan" to Destroy Israel

The PLO has since its birth been dedicated to the total destruction of the State of Israel. In analyzing the stunning military victories that Israel achieved against overwhelming Arab armies in 1948, 1967, and the October 1973 Yom Kippur War, many in the Arab leadership—both in the

PLO and in surrounding Arab states—concluded that they could never defeat Israel's superior armed forces through military action. Instead, the PLO leadership and its allies envisioned a three-stage strategy that would eventually result in Israel's destruction. The Phased Plan was formally adopted by the twelfth session of the Palestinian National Council in Cairo on June 9, 1974.

The plan contains three main points:

- Use "armed struggle" (terrorism) to establish an "independent combatant national authority" over any territory that is "liberated" from Israeli rule (Article 2).
- Continue the struggle against Israel, utilizing the newly acquired territory of the national authority as a base of terror operations (Article 4).
- Provoke an all-out war with Israel to encourage Arab neighbors to join the war to destroy the Jewish state (Article 8).[8]

Despite decades of negotiations and treaties between the Palestinians and Israel, the Phased Plan to destroy Israel remains the formal and actual political basis of all PLO actions and plans.[9] Significantly, Articles 5 and 6 of the PLO plan call for an armed revolution to overthrow the Jordanian monarchy and set up a new Palestinian leadership in Jordan that would ally itself with the Palestinian National Authority. The PLO has never recognized the legitimacy of the royal kingdom of Jordan as a nation independent from the rest of Palestine (Israel, the West Bank, and Gaza).

Before his death, Egyptian journalist Faysal al-Husseini wrote a revealing article published in the Egyptian newspaper *Al-'Arabi*. He declared that the Oslo Agreement with Israel was nothing less than a Trojan-horse attempt to destroy the Jewish state. "Had the U.S. and Israel not realized, before Oslo, that all that was left of the Palestinian National movement and the Pan-Arab movement was a wooden horse called Arafat or the PLO, they would never have opened their fortified gates and let it inside their walls."[10]

## The Defense of Israel

As Israel found herself surrounded by Arab nations committed to her destruction, she was forced to arm herself, spending some 30 percent of her gross national product on defense. (By comparison, the United States spends about 6 percent). The combined Arab forces that oppose Israel possess more tanks, artillery, and soldiers than the Russian military. It is a miracle that tiny Israel, only half the size of Switzerland and with a population of only six million, can stand against such an overwhelming array of military force.

Israel performs a key role in the coordinated military defense of both the Middle East and the southern defensive perimeter of North Atlantic Treaty Organization's (NATO) military theater. Without Israel's powerful air force and army, the United States would not be able to secure the Persian Gulf area unless it permanently committed a significant portion of its available armored units, as it is now doing temporarily in the war in Iraq.

Israel also provides the United States and NATO with tremendous amounts of vital intelligence on Russia, various Arab countries, and al Qaeda. Israel has given the United States technical data and even armaments from enemy nations, including Soviet M-62 tanks, SAM-9 missiles, and Mig-23 fighter jets. The Mossad, Israel's intelligence service, is judged by its competitors to be the best in the world. It has warned Saudi Arabia, Jordan, and Egypt of several planned assassinations and coup attempts against their leaders. Israel's electronic warfare technology is second to none in the world. Her sophisticated electronic and human intelligence penetration of terrorist plots has been of immense help to the West.

## Rising Anti-Semitism

Jesus Christ warned that one of the unmistakable signs of the return of the Messiah would be the rise of a terrible hatred of the Jews. "Then shall they deliver you up to be afflicted, and shall kill you: and ye shall be hated of all nations for my name's sake. And then shall many be offended, and shall betray one another, and shall hate one another" (Matthew 24:9–10). Even after the Holocaust killed more than six million Jews in Europe, we now see a brutal rise of anti-Semitism throughout the world.

This hatred of the Jewish people is the mark of a civilization unredeemed by the love of God. Satan inspired a growing hatred of the Jews in Germany that culminated in the Holocaust. The Nazi propaganda machine of Joseph Goebbels developed sophisticated cartoons and evil portrayals of the Jewish people to prepare German citizens to think of Jews as less than human. Today it is terrible to witness in Russia and Arab countries the same types of portrayals fomenting hatred of the Jews.

Satan hates the Jews because God selected Israel to be His chosen people. The Jews acted as God's messengers to mankind: receiving the Ten Commandments, the written Word of God, and receiving the Messiah through His birth to Mary. God changed Jacob's name to Israel, which means "Prince with God." Satan knows that God's plan for the redemption of humanity involves the redemption of His chosen people, Israel. The devil can read prophecy as well as we can. He knows the rebirth of Israel in 1948 began a chain of prophetic events that will end in his destruction by the supernatural power of Jesus the Messiah at Armageddon.

Christ's prophecy of a terrible persecution of Jews in the final generation is beginning to be fulfilled. Jewish synagogues and cemeteries are being desecrated around the world. Even in Japan, with less than a thousand Jews, hate-filled anti-Semitic books, including *The Protocols of the Elders of Zion,* are sold in bookstores and book kiosks. *The Protocols of the Elders of Zion* was forged by the anti-Semitic Russian czarist secret police prior to World War I. The book purports to be a plan by a group of Jewish conspirators to take over the world. Amazingly, even though numerous courts have documented that it is a forgery, this evil book continues to be a bestseller throughout the Arab world, Russia, and many other countries. Tragically, even some Christians have been deceived by it.

Sheikh Abdul Aziz Oudeh, one of the leaders of Islamic Jihad, gave an explicit anti-Semitic speech during an Islamic Committee for Palestine meeting held in Chicago in 1990. He declared, "Allah is bringing the Jews back to Palestine in large groups from all over the world to their big graveyard where the promise will be realized upon them and what was destined will be carried out."[11]

Arab children throughout the Middle East are taught from the nursery through high school that the Jews are the source of all the problems faced by the Arab people. Their parents, teachers, and imams have indoctrinated them since birth with a virulent hatred of the Jews, teaching that Jews are not really human but only the "children of pigs and monkeys."

Tragically, under extreme pressure to comply with the PLO, Palestinian Christian clergy, including Greek Orthodox, Roman Catholic, and Protestant, often refer publicly to Jews as "satanic." Although it is hard for most Western readers to accept, government-mandated or state-owned newspapers—even those in so-called moderate Arab nations such as Jordan, Egypt, or Saudi Arabia—constantly publish outrageous lies about the Jews, including the ancient blood libel that maintains that Jews kill Gentile children so they can use the blood to make the bread eaten at Passover.

## AL QAEDA'S DECLARATION OF WAR AGAINST THE WEST

While extreme Islam does all it can to destroy Israel and the democratic values of the West, values that guarantee every individual's freedom to practice the religion of his or her choice, all Islamist societies punish by death anyone who forsakes Islam.

The textbook *Islamic Culture* outlines the duty of all Muslims to execute anyone who chooses to leave the Islamic faith.

> The logical reason for executing a person who abandons Islam is the following: There is nothing in Islam that comes in contrast to human nature. Whoever joins Islam after recognizing its truth and after tasting its sweetness and then abandons it—is in fact rebelling against truth and logic. Like any other regime, Islam

has to protect itself; therefore this punishment [execution] awaits the person who abandons it, because he is spreading doubt about Islam....

Abandoning Islam is a crime that warrants a severe punishment... [The sequence of stages of the punishment are]:

   a. Urging [the sinner] to recant immediately.
   b. Warning him of the implications of his persistence in abandoning Islam, namely warning him that he will be executed.
   c. Executing the sinner if he persists in [his decision to] abandon Islam.[12]

### Bin Laden's Formal Declaration of War

Against such a backdrop, it's important to realize that Osama bin Laden has formalized a declaration of war against the West. In 1998 he and his associate commander, Ayman al-Zawahiri, issued a fatwa under the banner of the International Islamic Front for Jihad Against the Jews and Crusaders. The fatwa was published on February 23, 1998, in the Arabic newspaper *Al-Quds al-'Arabi.*

Bin Laden and al-Zawahiri were so offended by the presence of American "infidel" troops in Saudi Arabia, in the area of the holy cities of Mecca and Medina, that they declared:

> The ruling to kill the Americans and their allies—civilians and military—is an individual duty for every Muslim who can do it in any country in which it is possible to do it, in order to liberate the al-Aqsa Mosque and the holy mosque [Mecca] from their grip, and in order for their armies to move out of all the lands of Islam, defeated and unable to threaten any Muslim. This is in accordance with the words of Almighty God, "and fight the pagans all together as they fight you all together," and "fight

them until there is no more tumult or oppression, and there prevail justice and faith in God."[13]

It is significant that although all Western troops withdrew from Saudi Arabia in 2003, there has been no corresponding softening of the call for the worldwide annihilation of Christians and Jews.

## THE WORDS OF THE PROPHETS

Joel was referring to our own last-days generation when he declared:

> Proclaim ye this among the Gentiles; Prepare war, wake up the mighty men, let all the men of war draw near; let them come up: Beat your plowshares into swords, and your pruninghooks into spears: let the weak say, I am strong. Assemble yourselves, and come, all ye heathen, and gather yourselves together round about.... Come up to the valley of Jehoshaphat: for there will I sit to judge all the heathen round about. (Joel 3:9–12)

Joel prophesied that in the last days there would be a terrible attack on Jerusalem that would arouse its Jewish defenders to protect the population and destroy their enemies.

The prophet Zechariah prophesied more than two thousand years ago:

> Behold, I will make Jerusalem a cup of trembling unto all the people round about, when they shall be in the siege both against Judah and against Jerusalem.
>
> And in that day will I make Jerusalem a burdensome stone for all people: all that burden themselves with it shall be cut in pieces, though all the people of the earth be gathered together against it. (Zechariah 12:2–3)

In light of the overwhelming force of the armies assaulting Jerusalem, Ezekiel prophesied that God would use supernatural power to defend His Holy City. The Lord will utterly destroy the armies attempting to destroy the Jews who have returned to rebuild Zion (see Ezekiel 38–39).

The Arab and Islamic hatred for the Jews, which has continued unabated for millenniums, will culminate in a massive military invasion of the Jewish state. This invasion will involve the armed forces of a multitude of Islamic nations, led by the Russian military, and with many allied forces motivated by a deeply held anti-Semitism. In the next chapter we will explore the fascinating prophecies that describe this coming battle. The armies of many nations who seek to destroy God's chosen people will be destroyed, and it will happen exactly as the ancient prophets foretold.

# WILL THIS WAR SIGNAL THE LAST DAYS?

*Signs of the Coming War of Gog and Magog*

From the beginning of history, the narrow strip of land along the eastern shore of the Mediterranean, the Crescent, has been a strategic prize for every rising empire that sought to dominate the world. The empires of Egypt, Assyria, Babylon, Medo-Persia, Greece, and Rome all fought in turn to capture Israel. Empires seeking uncontested world power needed to conquer Israel to acquire or to control the strategic land bridge linking Europe, Asia, and Africa.

Today the land bridge is not as important for commerce and troop movement as it was before the advent of air transportation and large troop carriers. But strategists in Russia and those working for al Qaeda know that the conquest of Israel, the West's most reliable Middle Eastern military ally, would deliver the whole region into their control. Whoever controls the Middle East and the Persian Gulf oil supplies can set the agenda for Europe and Asia, including the rapidly growing economies of Japan, China, and India. All industrialized nations are dependent on the Middle East for critical energy supplies.

Israel is a crucial puzzle piece that completes the master plan for world domination, which explains why the land of Palestine is much sought after by both Islamists and the government of Russia. Because of Israel's superior military strength, a world power such as Russia is needed to ally with the Muslim armies in order to successfully invade Israel.

Such an assessment is not idle speculation. The prophet Ezekiel foretold in approximately 580 BC that Russia would lead a confederacy of nations to invade Israel:

> Son of man, set thy face against Gog, the land of Magog, the chief prince of Meshech and Tubal, and prophesy against him....
>
> After many days thou shalt be visited: in the latter years thou shalt come into the land that is brought back from the sword, and is gathered out of many people, against the mountains of Israel, which have been always waste: but it is brought forth out of the nations, and they shall dwell safely all of them....
>
> And thou shalt come from thy place out of the north parts, thou, and many people with thee, all of them riding upon horses, a great company, and a mighty army. (Ezekiel 38:2, 8, 15)

A confederacy of Russian and Islamic armies—including Eastern European countries, Iran, Sudan, Ethiopia, Libya, and the Arab nations—will attempt to capture the geographically vital area of Palestine. When I describe a military alliance made up of Islamic and Arab armies and headed by Russia, it raises the question of why Islamists would ally themselves with Russia. In past decades Muslim forces have battled the Russians in both Afghanistan and Chechnya. So why would Islamic nations now choose a former enemy as an ally? The Bible doesn't answer this question, but a very plausible explanation is that Russia and the Islamic enemies of Israel share a profound anti-Semitism. As we saw in the preceding chapter, hatred of Israel is on the rise and is prophesied in Scripture as a sign of the last days (see Matthew 24:9–10).

## IDENTIFYING MAGOG AS RUSSIA

In a prophecy that was given twenty-five centuries ago, God described a battle in which He would destroy the armies of Russia and its Islamic Arab and North African allies on the mountains of Israel. Today there are abundant signs that the stage is being set for the War of Gog and Magog.

> And the word of the LORD came unto me, saying, Son of man, set thy face against Gog, the land of Magog, the chief prince of Meshech and Tubal, and prophesy against him, and say, Thus saith the Lord GOD; Behold, I am against thee, O Gog, the chief prince of Meshech and Tubal: And I will turn thee back, and put hooks into thy jaws, and I will bring thee forth, and all thine army, horses and horsemen, all of them clothed with all sorts of armour, even a great company with bucklers and shields, all of them handling swords: Persia, Ethiopia, and Libya with them; all of them with shield and helmet: Gomer, and all his bands; the house of Togarmah of the north quarters, and all his bands: and many people with thee. (Ezekiel 38:1–6)

Since many of the nations named in this prophecy are no longer identified as such, we need to explore which modern-day countries are counted among the invading armies. Following the flood in Noah's day, his sons and grandsons dispersed to various parts of Asia, Europe, and Africa. Genesis 10 records the ancient genealogy of the nations, naming the tribes that Ezekiel identifies in his end-time prophecy. Ancient historians, including Herodotus and Flavius Josephus in his *Antiquities of the Jews,* tell us where most of the tribes ultimately settled. Many Jewish and Christian scholars conclude that the tribes referred to by Ezekiel are found in the list of nations that follows. This chart shows the ancient name of each tribe and the modern nation that now occupies that particular territory.

## NATIONS MENTIONED IN EZEKIEL 38:1–6

| THE ANCIENT NATIONS | THE MODERN NATIONS |
|---|---|
| Gog and Magog | Russia |
| Meshech and Tubal | Somewhere in Russia |
| Persia | Iran, Iraq, Afghanistan |
| Ethiopia | Ethiopia and Sudan |
| Libya | Libya |
| Gomer | Eastern Europe |
| Togarmah | Southeastern Europe, Turkey |
| "Many people with thee" | Various other nations allied with Russia |

Arab writers confirm that in the Arabic language, the name for the Great Wall of China is "the wall of Al Magog," because the wall was built to keep out the invading armies from Magog (Russia).[1] Magog is a real nation occupying a territory that was known to Ezekiel and his Jewish readers in the fifth century before Christ. I believe the evidence supports the conclusion that Magog refers to the territory that is currently occupied by Russia. The majority of prophecy teachers agree with this conclusion. However, some biblical scholars have suggested that the name Magog was connected with small tribal groups in ancient Mesopotamia in the area presently occupied by Iran.

## JEWISH SCHOLARSHIP IDENTIFIES MAGOG

The prophecies in Ezekiel 38 were studied for thousands of years by Jewish sages. Consequently, the conclusions drawn by these scholars illuminate the true meaning of the Hebrew words *Gog* and *Magog*. Genesis 10 lists

Magog as a grandson of Noah who ultimately gave birth to a nation. The name Magog was well known to every Jew who studied this passage yearly as part of the Sabbath schedule of reading through the Torah each year. The prophet Ezekiel named Magog along with other specific allied nations, such as Libya, Persia, and Ethiopia. This strongly suggests that Ezekiel expected the name Magog to be understood by his Jewish readers as a real nation, not as an abstract symbol of evil.

A recent commentary on Genesis, *Bereishis—Genesis: A New Translation with a Commentary Anthologized from Talmudic, Midrashic and Rabbinic Sources,* includes the following commentary on Genesis 10:2: "Magog is mentioned several times in Scripture, e.g. Ezekiel 38:2; 39:6 as the name of the land of Gog. Kesses HaSofer identifies them with the Mongols who lived near China, for in fact the very name Mongol is a corruption of Magog."[2]

The commentary also cites Arab writers who refer to the Great Wall of China as the "wall of Al Magog." In *The Pentateuch and Haftorahs,* Dr. J. H. Hertz, the late chief rabbi of the British Empire, comments on the famous Genesis 10 passage: "Magog—The Scythians, whose territory lay on the borders of the Caucasus."[3] The Caucasus is a mountain range in western Russia. Another credible scholar, the Jewish-Christian writer Dr. Alfred Edersheim, in his book *Bible History—Old Testament* identified Magog as the Scythians.

A fascinating commentary on Daniel identifies Magog with these words:

> The various traditions concerning the identity of Magog, who in Genesis 10:2 is listed among the sons of Noah's son Japheth, tend to place the land of Magog in what today is southeastern Russia—the Caucasian region, which lies between the Black and Caspian seas....
>
> This is in agreement with *Yerushalmi Megillah* 3:9, which renders Magog as... *the Goths,* a group of nomadic tribes who destroyed the Scythians and made their homes in Scythian territory....

Our identification of Magog as Caucasia, which was at one time inhabited by the Goths, is based on the assumption that the land of Magog is named after Japheth's son.[4]

Southern Russia occupies this area today.

The Jewish historian Flavius Josephus, who lived at the time of the apostle Paul, wrote a definitive history of the Jewish people called *Antiquities of the Jews.* Josephus identified the people from Magog as what is today Russia: "Magog founded those that from him were named Magogites, but who are by the Greeks called Scythians."[5]

The section of Young's *Analytical Concordance to the Holy Bible* dealing with Magog speaks of ancient Scythia or Tartar, a name used to describe southern Russia in past centuries. Young said that the name Gog was derived from a phrase that meant a "high mountain" and that the word "Gog" in Ezekiel 38 referred to "Scythia in the north of Asia."[6]

Arno C. Gaebelein in his book *The Prophet Ezekiel* wrote on the identification of Magog:

Magog's land, was located in, what is called today, the Caucasus and the adjoining steppes. And the three Rosh, Meshech and Tubal were called by the ancients Scythians. They roamed as nomads in the country around and north of the Black and the Caspian Seas, and were known as the wildest barbarians.[7]

## THE COMING INVASION

The prophet described an invasion that would come without warning in which the enemy invades like a "storm" or "cloud to cover the land" (Ezekiel 38:9). It is possible that the prophet saw in a vision an airborne invasion force, like D day, and used the best words he had available to describe such an event.

Ezekiel prophesied that the leader of the invading force would describe the military action with these words: "I will go up to the land of unwalled villages; I will go to them that are at rest, that dwell safely, all of them dwelling without walls, and having neither bars nor gates" (Ezekiel 38:11). It is interesting to note that during the lifetime of Ezekiel and up until 1900, virtually all of the villages and cities in the Middle East had walls for defense. Ezekiel had never seen a village or city without defensive walls. Yet, in our day, Israel is a "land of unwalled villages" for the simple reason that modern techniques of warfare (bombs and missiles) make city walls irrelevant for defense. This is one more indication that his prophecy refers to our modern generation.

Aside from Russia, it would be difficult to name any other nation to the north of Israel capable of leading such a huge confederacy of Arab and North African nations. For the last five decades Russia has trained the military officers and intelligence staff of all the nations listed in Ezekiel's prophecy. The phrases "prepare for thyself" and "be thou a guard unto them" in Ezekiel 38:7 could indicate Russia's future role in providing arms and military leadership to the confederacy of invading nations. The armories of the nations that oppose Israel, without exception, are filled with AK47 assault rifles, surface-to-air missiles, RPG7 antitank weapons, and massive amounts of other Russian-manufactured arms—exactly as the Bible foretold.

## THE WAR OF GOG AND MAGOG

And it shall come to pass at the same time when Gog shall come against the land of Israel, saith the Lord GOD, that my fury shall come up in my face. For in my jealousy and in the fire of my wrath have I spoken, Surely in that day there shall be a great shaking in the land of Israel.… And I will call for a sword against him [Gog] throughout all my mountains, saith the Lord GOD: every man's sword shall be against his brother. (Ezekiel 38:18–19, 21)

Apart from the strategic and economic motivations to control the Middle East, the final reason Russia will attack Israel is because God will supernaturally put the thought of her conquest into the Russian leader's mind. Ezekiel prophetically identified the Russian leader as "Gog" because of his connection to "Magog," the name of ancient Russia. The only other occasion in the Bible where we find God overriding a man's mind is detailed in Exodus. God used the Egyptian Pharaoh's refusal to free the Israelites as an opportunity to demonstrate His power and sovereignty through the series of ten plagues. When Pharaoh finally agreed to release the Hebrew slaves, God established His divine power by miraculously delivering His people from slavery.

Similarly, in our day, God has determined to reveal His power to deliver His chosen people from their enemies by destroying the Russian and Islamic armies. It will not be Israel's brilliant military abilities or America's weapons that will save the children of Israel in their greatest hour of need. God will intervene supernaturally in a way that He has not done since the days of Moses.

✓ The Lord will unleash the greatest earthquake ever felt as a response to the attack of the Russian and Islamic armies. Though focused on the mountains of Israel, God declares that "all the men that are upon the face of the earth, shall shake at my presence, and the mountains shall be thrown down, and the steep places shall fall, and every wall shall fall to the ground" (Ezekiel 38:20). God will sow confusion between the various components of Magog's armies. As the prophet declared, "I will call for a sword against him throughout all my mountains, saith the Lord GOD: every man's sword shall be against his brother" (Ezekiel 38:21). Several times in biblical history, God has caused confusion in the minds of enemy armies so that they mistakenly attacked their own soldiers.

The prophet gave additional details describing how God will defeat the invading forces: "I will plead against him with pestilence and with blood; and I will rain upon him, and upon his bands, and upon the many people that are with him, an overflowing rain, and great hailstones, fire, and brimstone" (Ezekiel 38:22). These supernatural weapons will create the greatest military disaster in history, with some 85 percent of the enemies' soldiers left dead on the field of battle (see Ezekiel 39:2). The hailstones, fire, confusion, earthquake, and plague will defeat the invading armies in the mountains of Israel.

The numbers of the dead will be so overwhelming that it will take seven months for Israel to bury the bodies in a valley east of the Dead Sea in Jordan. In Scripture, it is called "Hamongog," the valley of the multitude of Russia (see Ezekiel 39:11–12). The Bible declares that the invaders' weapons and fuel won't be wasted. "They that dwell in the cities of Israel shall go forth, and shall set on fire and burn the weapons...and they shall burn them with fire seven years" (Ezekiel 39:9). Many Russian weapons and fuel depots will provide fuel to burn in the years following God's victory.

We live in the most complacent and atheistic generation in history. But when God defeats this awesome invasion force with His display of miraculous power, many people will repent of their sinful rebellion and unbelief. The Lord declares, "I will set my glory among the heathen, and all the heathen shall see my judgment that I have executed, and my hand that I have laid upon them. So the house of Israel shall know that I am the LORD their God from that day forward" (Ezekiel 39:21–22).

When the citizens of the Gentile nations see the devastation of the Russian and Islamic armies, they will know that God is the Lord of Israel. The Jews in Israel will also know that God has saved them from the hands of their enemies. With Israel saved from destruction, the stage will be set for the rebuilding of the Temple in Jerusalem and the rise of the Antichrist in Europe. Russia and her Eastern European allies will be militarily devastated. The power vacuum will be filled by the rising colossus of a reunited Europe (a revived Roman Empire) under the dynamic leadership of the coming prince of darkness.

The silence of Bible prophecy about America's future role in end-time events suggests that something will occur that will prevent the United States from continuing to act as the world's leading superpower. Possibly the resurrection of all believers, an economic collapse, or a series of devastating WMD terrorist attacks will force the United States to retreat to "Fortress North America" and refuse to be the world's policeman. Only time will tell.

## WHEN WILL THE WAR OF GOG AND MAGOG TAKE PLACE?

The War of God and Magog will signal the unfolding of God's plans for the last days. But there is much debate about the timing of the war in relation to other known end-time events. Prophecy scholars disagree on when the war will take place in relation to the seven years of the Great Tribulation. They also disagree on the relation of the War of Gog and Magog to the battle of Armageddon. Some believe the two wars refer to the *same* battle. Others insist that they are two different wars, separated by at least seven years. Let's look at each of the most prominent views and then explore which interpretation has the most biblical warrant.

Some prophecy teachers conclude that the War of Gog and Magog—the Russo-Arab invasion of Israel—will occur during the Tribulation, the seven-year treaty period leading up to the battle of Armageddon. But after many years of careful study, I am convinced that the burden of prophetic evidence points to the War of Magog occurring at some point in the near future, prior to the Antichrist making his seven-year treaty with Israel.

When examining the timing of the War of Gog and Magog, we need to consider three possibilities. The war could take place (1) prior to Daniel's seventieth week of years and the seven-year treaty of the Antichrist with Israel or (2) at some point during the seven-year treaty period or (3) at the end of the seven-year treaty period as part of the battle of Armageddon. My reasons for rejecting the second and third time frames are that they would demand that the invading forces attack Israel during the time when the Antichrist is reigning as the false messiah, the world dictator, and while he is committed by his seven-year "covenant" (see Daniel 9:27) to defend Israel against her enemies.

The detailed description of this war in Ezekiel 38–39 does not mention the Antichrist, the revived Roman Empire, its armies, the seven-year treaty, or the Jews' expectations that anyone will be obliged to protect them from the invading Russian and Islamic armies. I find it inconceivable that the Antichrist would not be mentioned either as Israel's defender or her betrayer if this invasion occurs during the seven-year period when he is sworn to defend Israel (see Daniel 9:24–27).

Additionally, it is difficult to see how the War of Gog and Magog in Ezekiel 38–39 could be part of the battle of Armageddon, because all the details of that battle as described in Joel 2, Zechariah 12–14, and the book of Revelation differ significantly regarding the methods, the armaments, the identities of the armies, and the ultimate destruction of the enemy forces described by Ezekiel. The prophet tells us that "they shall burn them [Magog's weapons] with fire seven years" for fuel and "seven months shall the house of Israel be burying of them, that they may cleanse the land" (see Ezekiel 39:9, 12). If this war was part of the battle of Armageddon, it seems unlikely that it would take seven months to cleanse the land of bodies or that the Jews would have to use Russian weapons for fuel for seven years during the miraculous prosperity of Christ's millennial rule, which will follow the battle of Armageddon.

The main reason some prophecy scholars have concluded that the War of Gog and Magog takes place during the seven-year treaty with the Antichrist is because they believe that Ezekiel 38:11–12 tells us that the prophesied war occurs at a time when Israel appears to be at peace. The prophet declares that Gog, the military leader of Russia, will say, "I will go up to the land of unwalled villages; I will go to them that are at rest, that dwell safely, all of them dwelling without walls, and having neither bars nor gates, to take a spoil." Certain scholars have concluded that this description refers to a peaceful time for Israel and that it must occur during the first part of the seven-year defensive treaty with the Antichrist.

The first problem with such an interpretation is that Ezekiel does not mention the seven-year treaty or any expectation by Israel that the Antichrist's kingdom will protect them. Second, Ezekiel's reference to "dwell safely" and "without walls…neither bars nor gates" refers precisely to Israel's current military situation, where she is dwelling safely because of her strong armed defense and where her cities and villages have no walls or defensive bars. The prophet had never seen a city without walls, so he was astonished when he saw, in a vision, Israel dwelling in the future without walls. Ezekiel lived in a time when every city in the world used huge walls for military defense.

Israel relies on swift counterattacks and mobile defenses and therefore does not surround even her West Bank settlements with walls. In this analysis we should realize that Israel's security fence against suicide bombers is 96 percent an electronic fence with wires and sensors, and only 4 percent is constructed of a concrete barrier to block the vision of Palestinian snipers shooting from the West Bank into Israeli territory.

The prophecies in Ezekiel 38–39 constitute the most detailed description of a future war found in Scripture. The prophet describes in great detail the weapons used, the nations fighting on both sides, the sequence of developments in the battle, and God's supernatural destruction of Israel's enemies. However, if this battle took place within the seven years leading to Armageddon, I believe the prophet would refer either to the Antichrist's response to the violation of his treaty or to his betrayal of Israel by refusing to protect her against this military assault. Ezekiel's prophecy is silent as to the role of the Antichrist. Ezekiel also does not mention the role of the Messiah, who will be another central figure in the events leading to the battle of Armageddon. This silence convinces me that the War of Gog and Magog must occur before the Antichrist arises to conclude his fateful seven-year treaty with the Jews.

Further, Ezekiel's vision does not demand that Israel actually live at total peace with her Arab neighbors prior to this prophesied attack but rather that she is not living in fear of immediate attack (see Ezekiel 38:8). The Bible assures us that Israel and the nations will not find true peace until the Messiah, the Prince of Peace, returns to the earth. Israel will remain an armed camp surrounded by enemies committed to her destruction until God changes the hearts of mankind. So Ezekiel's phrase "dwell safely" may simply indicate that Israel will not expect an attack in the immediate future, perhaps because of ongoing negotiations, such as the Middle East peace negotiations being conducted as this chapter is written. Ezekiel's description could easily apply to the conditions that exist today.

I believe the War of Gog and Magog will occur before the seven-year treaty. It will create the preconditions that will allow the Antichrist to consolidate his revived Roman Empire in Europe.

When the devastating War of Gog and Magog is concluded, the Bible states that God "will send a fire on Magog, and among them that dwell carelessly in the isles: and they shall know that I am the LORD" (Ezekiel 39:6). With the Russo-Islamic armies 85 percent destroyed ("I will turn thee back, and leave but the sixth part of thee" [Ezekiel 39:2]), the world's political and military balance of power will be profoundly altered.

## THE COMING TRIBULATION

The prophet explains God's motive in allowing the defeat of the invading armies. "Thus I will magnify myself, and sanctify myself; and I will be known in the eyes of many nations, and they shall know that I am the LORD" (Ezekiel 38:23). When the miraculous battle is over, Israel and all the Gentile nations will know that it was the power of God that destroyed the invading armies. There will be few atheists left in the world after His supernatural intervention to save Israel. This tremendous victory will set the stage for the Great Tribulation and the coming Messiah.

The War of Gog and Magog is the key event that will set the stage for the completion of God's prophetic program to establish His Messianic kingdom. With Russia and the vast Islamic armies destroyed, Europe will finally be able to complete its unification plans. There will be a time of peace in which Israel will finally be able to build the Third Temple in the area north of the Dome of the Rock. The Jewish sages believed the War of Gog and Magog would usher in the Messianic era. They wrote that the return of the prophet Elijah would occur before the War of Gog and Magog.[8]

There is an oral tradition recorded from the *Vilna Gaon,* a Jewish commentary, that points out the significance of the Russian navy (Magog) passing through the Bosporus straits on the way to the Mediterranean through the Dardanelles: "It is now the time to put on your Sabbath clothes because the Messiah is coming."[9] The Jewish sages warned that the generation that witnessed Magog's (Russia's) preparations to invade Israel should prepare its heart for the Messiah.

"Behold, it is come, and it is done, saith the Lord GOD; this is the day whereof I have spoken" (Ezekiel 39:8). God's appointment with Russia and its Islamic allies is set; the appointment will be kept.

When the Gog and Magog invasion occurs, it appears that the only response from the Western democracies will be a diplomatic protest. Ezekiel 38:13 says that "Sheba, and Dedan, and the merchants of Tarshish, with all the young lions thereof [probably the United Kingdom, the United States, and the British Commonwealth nations], shall say unto thee, Art thou come to take a spoil?" Tarshish, Sheba, and Dedan were ancient trading nations and are believed by many Bible scholars to refer to Great Britain and her former colonies ("the young lions thereof"). It will not be the West that responds to this unprovoked attack. The superpower that intervenes to save Israel in her greatest hour of need will be her great Defender, the God of Abraham. The Islamic nations will realize that God has intervened against them, and they will reluctantly accept that this is not the time when they will achieve victory over their Jewish enemies.

The Lord's total defeat of the Russo-Islamic armies will create the political, military, and religious conditions that will lead the Jews to rebuild their beloved Temple in Jerusalem. In the next chapter, we will examine the remarkable preparations that are now under way for the rebuilding of the holy Temple, as prophesied throughout the Word of God.

# A New Temple for the Last Days

*Developments That Will Set the Stage for the Antichrist*

Almost two thousand years ago the brutally efficient legions of Rome destroyed Jerusalem and burned the beautiful Temple to the ground. The Temple was leveled on the ninth day of Av (August) in AD 70, and it remains in ruins after two millenniums. But it won't always be this way. God declared that the Temple will be rebuilt in the generation that witnesses the return of the Jews to their Promised Land. That generation also will see the return of the Messiah.

In biblical times, a generation was considered to be forty years, but life spans have greatly increased since the first century, so most of those who were very young during the 1948 War of Independence are still alive. However, many scholars doubt that the Temple will be rebuilt due to the immense practical and political obstacles that stand in the way. One of the greatest obstacles is that the Jews cannot rebuild the Temple or resume their worship in the Temple, as required in Micah 4:1–2, unless the ancient Sanhedrin is reconvened. As the highest sacred body of Jewish lawmakers, the Sanhedrin must exist in order to reestablish the Levitical priesthood.

And beyond the reinstituting of the Sanhedrin and the priesthood, there are additional challenges: refashioning the utensils of Temple worship, determining the correct location on which to rebuild the Temple, and addressing the political and religious strife that surrounds the Temple Mount.

For thousands of years the Jews have mourned the burning of Solomon's Temple on the ninth day of the month Av (August) in 587 BC. On this solemn day every year, Jews read the tragic passage from the book of Lamentations that describes the destruction. Righteous Jews mourn the loss of their holy sanctuary, where God communed with them from the Holy of Holies. After the Roman army burned the Second Temple in AD 70 on the very same day, the ninth of Av, the Temple was lost as the center of Israel's spiritual life. The religious life of Israel turned to the local synagogue, the Torah, and the rabbinical commentary writings of the Talmud. With these three, Jews continued to express their love for God's holy name.

However, the Lord prophesied that the Jewish exiles would, in the last days, return to the Promised Land to rebuild the Temple (see Revelation 11:1–2). The abandoned cities that had been in ruins for thousands of years would also be rebuilt. During nineteen centuries of exile, the Jews repeatedly prayed to return to the Promised Land. Each year on Tisha B'Av, the ninth of Av, they prayed, "Next year in Jerusalem." Together with the hope of returning to the Holy Land, religious Jews have longed for the rebuilding of the Temple and the establishment of the long-promised kingdom of God under the rule of the coming Messiah. They prayed earnestly to God, "May it be Thy will that the Temple be speedily rebuilt in our days." This ancient prayer was repeated three times each day in the hope that the Lord would return His supernatural glory, the Shekinah presence, to the Temple rebuilt in their generation. After twenty centuries of waiting, the current generation has been given the task of making the ancient dreams come true.

# THE SECOND TEMPLE

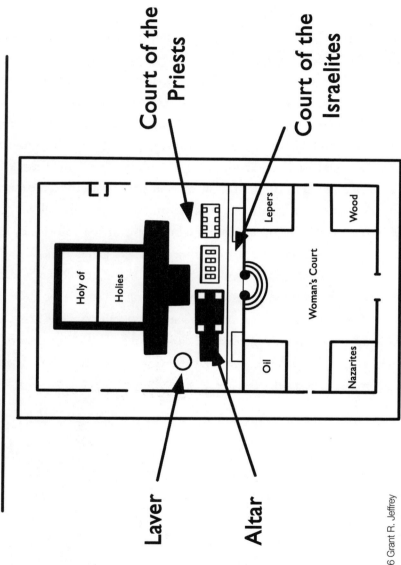

Court of the Priests

Court of the Israelites

Holy of Holies

Lepers

Wood

Woman's Court

Oil

Nazarites

Laver

Altar

## "LET THEM MAKE ME A SANCTUARY THAT I MAY DWELL AMONG THEM"

The greatest Jewish rabbi, Moses Maimonides, also known as Rambam (circa AD 1200), taught that the intense study of the Temple and its worship rituals was of eternal significance to Jews of every generation because it revealed the nature of God and His eternal relationship to Israel. Maimonides noted that the 613 *mitzvot,* or separate commandments, found in the Torah also include the direct command of God to the Jews to build the Temple. "And let them make me a sanctuary; that I may dwell among them. According to all that I show thee, after the pattern of the tabernacle, and the pattern of all the instruments thereof, even so shall ye make it" (Exodus 25:8–9). Maimonides noted that this divine commandment was never rescinded, and thus it still applied to every generation.

Three thousand years ago God revealed to King David and his son Solomon the detailed plans for the building of the Temple on Mount Moriah in Jerusalem—not only the structure but also the items used in worship. The worship instruments and vessels, including the ark of the covenant, were modeled after the pattern of the sacred objects in the eternal Temple in heaven.

## ✓ PROPHECIES OF THE THIRD TEMPLE

God has promised repeatedly that the Temple will be rebuilt in the last days. These prophecies include predictions by Amos (750 BC), Micah (740 BC), and Haggai (520 BC):

> In that day will I raise up the tabernacle of David that is
> fallen, and close up the breaches thereof; and I will raise
> up his ruins, and I will build it as in the days of old.
> (Amos 9:11)

But in the last days it shall come to pass, that the mountain of the house of the LORD shall be established in the top of the mountains, and it shall be exalted above the hills; and people shall flow unto it. (Micah 4:1)

The glory of this latter house shall be greater than the former, saith the LORD of hosts. (Haggai 2:9)

Daniel prophesied twenty-five hundred years ago that the Temple would be rebuilt and would serve as the center of Israel's worship and sacrifice in the generation when the Messiah would return. In Daniel's famous vision of the seventy weeks (see Daniel 9:24–27), he predicted that the last great world dictator would arise from the revived Roman Empire and would conclude a seven-year peace treaty with Israel. After only three and a half years, the world leader would arbitrarily violate the seven-year treaty; at that time he would enter the rebuilt Temple and "he shall cause the sacrifice and the oblation to cease" (Daniel 9:27).

Obviously, the Antichrist cannot stop the daily sacrifice from occurring (Daniel 12:11) unless, prior to that moment, the Corban—the Levitical daily sacrificial system—has been reinstated. The daily sacrifice of sheep has not been practiced since the summer of AD 70, when the Romans burned the Second Temple. Before Daniel's prophecy can be fulfilled, the Jews must reinstate the ancient Levitical sacrificial system on the altar on the Temple Mount.

Jesus spoke to His disciples about the Great Tribulation under the coming Antichrist. He warned the Jews that "when ye therefore shall see the abomination of desolation, spoken of by Daniel the prophet, stand in the holy place, (whoso readeth, let him understand:) then let them which be in Judea flee into the mountains" (Matthew 24:15–16).

The "abomination of desolation" refers to Satan defiling the Holy Place in the Temple in the last three and a half years of the seven-year Tribulation.

The false prophet, the partner of the Antichrist, will then demand that the Antichrist be worshiped as "God" in the Temple. Christ's prophecy clearly suggests that the Temple first must be rebuilt so that the prophecy of the abomination of desolation can be fulfilled.

The apostle Paul advised in his second letter to the church at Thessalonica that the Lord Jesus Christ will not return in glory to set up His kingdom until "that man of sin," the Antichrist, is revealed. Paul describes the Antichrist as "the son of perdition; who opposeth and exalteth himself above all that is called God, or that is worshipped; so that he as God sitteth in the temple of God, showing himself that he is God" (2 Thessalonians 2:3–4).

Since the Six-Day War in 1967, Israel has controlled the entire city of Jerusalem for the first time in nineteen hundred years. Israel allows Muslim authorities to control religious activities and to police (without firearms) the Temple Mount with its Muslim shrine, the Dome of the Rock. Religious Jews don't worship in the area of the dome because the chief rabbis warn they might inadvertently trespass on the site of the Holy of Holies. Muslim control of the Temple Mount is thereby fulfilling the prophecy of Luke 21:24 that "Jerusalem shall be trodden down of the Gentiles, until the times of the Gentiles be fulfilled."

While Israel has demonstrated her willingness to allow Arabs full legal rights as citizens with access to all the sacred sites, the Arabs are adamant that the Jews and Christians will not have similar freedom to worship in Palestinian-controlled areas.

Israel, and especially the city of Jerusalem with its sacred Temple Mount, is the center of the world's major spiritual, political, and military conflict. The Bible prophesies that the final battle for the soul and destiny of mankind will be decided in Jerusalem, the "city of peace" and the future throne of the Messiah. Prophecy reveals that in our own generation we will witness the battle of Armageddon, the climactic final struggle for the destiny of mankind to be waged in the valley in front of the mount of Megiddo.

Current developments are laying the foundation for the coming Messianic kingdom of Jesus Christ. A significant development is that the Temple Institute, located in the Old City of Jerusalem, has completed a research project in preparation for the rebuilding of the Temple. In addition, the Orthodox Jewish religious leadership in Israel is awakening to the need to prepare the way for the rebuilding of the Third Temple.[1]

At the end of the dramatic Jewish victory over the Arab armies in the Six-Day War in June 1967, Israeli defense minister Gen. Moshe Dayan went to the Al-Aqsa Mosque for a significant meeting with the five leaders of the Supreme Muslim Council (the *Waqf*). This Islamic council controlled the Temple Mount during twenty years of Jordanian military rule over Jerusalem, from 1948 until the city's liberation by Israel's Defense Forces in early June 1967. The discussion between Dayan and the Supreme Muslim Council established Israel's religious and political policy concerning the Temple Mount, a policy that remains unchanged today. Dayan, a nonreligious Jew, did not understand the significance of the sacred Temple Mount for Israel, so he relinquished control of the area to the Arabs in the vain hope that his generous gesture would be appreciated. Unfortunately, despite the spectacular victory by the outnumbered Israeli Defense Forces in the Six-Day War, the Muslim Arabs interpreted Dayan's surrender of the most sacred site of the Jews as an indication of Israel's weakness of resolve.

Dayan ordered the Israeli flag removed from the Dome of the Rock, and his further concessions surrendered administrative control of the Temple Mount to the Supreme Muslim Council. Though Jews would be permitted limited access to the mount, all prayer by Jews and Christians was strictly prohibited. Thus Dayan rejected any public Jewish identification with the most sacred site of ancient Israel. Tragically for Dayan and many of Israel's subsequent nonreligious political and military leaders, the Temple Mount was thought to hold no significance except its historical importance. This failure by nonreligious Israeli leaders to demand control of the Temple Mount was the first in a long series of decisions that relinquished vital territory and religious rights. Their lack of faith in the God of Abraham and His prophecies in the Bible left them inadequately prepared to understand their enemies' deadly goals and the powerful divine promises and spiritual resources available to Israel in this life-and-death struggle.

Unlike Israel's secular leaders over the years, who often ignored the importance of God's prophecies, today there are groups of Israelis moving forward with plans in accordance with what God has revealed about the last days.

## THE THIRD TEMPLE

The Jewish scholar Maimonides wrote the fourteen-volume *Mishneh Torah,* which concluded with a volume called *Hilchos Bais HaBechirah* ("The Laws of God's Chosen House"). The book contains six mitzvot, or commandments, that summarize the Lord's laws given to Israel regarding the Temple:

1. The Jews are to build a sanctuary.
2. They are to build the altar with stone that is not hewn.
3. They are not to ascend the altar with steps; they must use a ramp.
4. They must fear and reverence the Temple.
5. They must guard the Temple completely.
6. They must never cease watching over the Temple.[2]

Maimonides declared that the Temple had two distinct purposes. The Temple's fundamental purpose was to reveal the divine presence, the glory of God, to mankind. The second purpose was to be the prescribed place, chosen by God, for the offering of divine sacrifices as outlined in the book of Exodus: "Speak unto the children of Israel, that they bring me an offering: of every man that giveth it willingly with his heart ye shall take my offering" (Exodus 25:2).

Rabbi Eliyahu Touger wrote the translation of Maimonides's *Mishneh Torah.* In his introduction to the fourteenth volume, Touger wrote, "As the text was being composed, we would frequently tell each other: 'Work faster. At any moment, Moshiach may come and rebuild the Temple. Who knows how this book will sell then?'"[3]

In 1948, Israel's chief rabbi ruled that, with the establishment of the Jewish state and the ingathering of the exiles, "the age of redemption" had begun. Today many of Israel's religious leaders are convinced that the Jews' repeated victories over Arab enemies have taken Judaism well beyond that point.[4] Says historian Israel Eldad, "We are at the stage where David was when he liberated Jerusalem; from that time until the construction of the Temple of Solomon, only one generation passed, so will it be with us."[5]

God gave King David a blueprint of the Temple that contained a Court of the Gentiles, which was in both Solomon's Temple and the Second Temple, built after the Jewish exiles returned from Babylon. In addition, Zechariah prophesied about the millennial Temple and kingdom: "And it shall come to pass, that every one that is left of all the nations which came against Jerusalem shall even go up from year to year to worship the King, the LORD of hosts, and to keep the feast of tabernacles" (Zechariah 14:16). These passages reveal that the Temple was to be a place of worship for both the Jews and the Gentiles who would join the Jews to worship God forever, following the establishment of the kingdom of God on earth by Jesus Christ.

In the near future, a dramatic change must occur in the political and religious leadership of Israel to allow the rebuilding of the Temple. What would motivate modern-day Israel to overcome the many significant obstacles to rebuilding the Temple? I believe it will be Israel's recognition of the defeat of extreme Islam through the supernatural act of God in the coming War of Gog and Magog. In addition, the recovery of the long-lost ark of the covenant would provide a powerful incentive since the original purpose of both the Tabernacle and the Temple was to provide a sacred house for the holy ark. Jeremiah 3:16 suggests that when the Messiah returns, Israel will stop visiting the ark of the covenant. This prophecy strongly suggests that at some point prior to Christ's return, the ark will be restored to Israel and will be a focus of the people's worship. But once Jesus rules from the throne of David in Jerusalem, the ark will no longer be the major focus of worship, as Christ will rule as King of kings.

## Could the Temple Be Rebuilt?

Talk about the rebuilding of the Temple inevitably brings up the related question: how could Israel legally or practically replace the existing structure known as the Dome of the Rock? This beautiful building was completed by Caliph Abdal-Malik on the Temple Mount in 691. For almost thirteen centuries most people have believed that this Muslim prayer shrine was built directly over the site of the original Temple. If this were the case, it would be difficult, if not impossible, to envision a situation in which Israel would be able to rebuild the Temple, which must be built exactly where the first two Temples stood.

Since 1948, Israel has been extremely protective of the religious sites of both the Muslims and the Christians, despite the fact that both of these religions have destroyed ancient Jewish holy buildings. This Jewish sensitivity to the Islamic veneration for the sacred Dome of the Rock led Israel to allow Muslims to retain a legal guardianship role over the Temple Mount, even after Israel conquered all of Jerusalem in 1967. Under the legal principle of status quo as practiced by the Turkish Ottoman Empire and the British Empire, all preexisting legal and religious rights were strictly maintained. Israel has enforced the same principle since 1948 in protecting each religion's historical rights and privileges.

Many Israelis today feel that allowing Muslim authorities to exercise administrative control over the Dome of the Rock and the Temple Mount was a tremendous error in political judgment. However, even this decision was the fulfillment of a nineteen-hundred-year-old prophecy made by John in the book of Revelation. In a vision of the final Tribulation period of three and a half years leading up to the battle of Armageddon, John is told by the angel, "Rise, and measure the temple of God, and the altar, and them that worship therein. But the court which is without the temple leave out, and measure it not; for it is given unto the Gentiles: and the holy city shall they tread under foot forty and two months" (Revelation 11:1–2).

John predicts that there will be a period after the rebuilding of the Temple and the sacrificial altar in which a large part of the Temple Mount known as the Court of the Gentiles (the court that is outside the Temple) will remain under the control of the Gentiles (Arab Muslims) for forty-two months, until Christ returns to set up His millennial kingdom.

### New Findings on the Temple's Exact Site

The rebuilding of the Temple has awaited the completion of recent archaeological research on and under the Temple Mount. Archaeological work indicates that the site of Solomon's Temple, and therefore the location for the future Temple, is in the open area of the Temple Mount directly north of the Dome of the Rock and directly opposite the sealed Eastern Gate, in an east-west line.

After the recapture of the Temple Mount in June 1967, Israeli archaeologists began to dig a nine-hundred-yard-long tunnel in a northerly direction along the Western Wall, beginning from the area known as Wilson's Arch to the northwest corner of the ancient Temple Mount. This tunnel is almost sixty-five yards below the level of the present-day streets of the Muslim quarter of the Old City of Jerusalem. It has become known as the Rabbi's Tunnel because, after 1967, the rabbis used it to approach as closely as possible the site of the Holy of Holies to conduct services and prayers.

Wilson's Arch is an opening to the immediate north of the Western Wall plaza, which forms the southern portion of the Western Wall of the thirty-five-acre Temple Mount. As I walked through the underground area where the Orthodox Jews keep their Torah scrolls, I saw where archaeologists had excavated to expose the original, massive, Herodian foundation stones. Some of these carved limestone foundation blocks are forty-six feet by ten feet by ten feet. They weigh up to four hundred tons each and are fitted so closely and perfectly together that it is impossible to insert even a razor blade between them. In comparison, the largest stones used in the Great Pyramid seldom exceeded fifty tons.

Farther along the tunnel, researchers uncovered a gate several hundred feet north of Wilson's Arch. The gate originally led into the Temple Mount and was built in the time of the Second Temple. The Jewish Mishnah records that the Western Gate led directly into the Beautiful Gate of the Second Temple. Now, after almost two thousand years, the Western Gate has been discovered.

This subterranean Western Gate was obstructed by rocks and debris from the destruction of the Second Temple by the Roman army in AD 70. As the debris was cleared away, it was discovered that this gate led to a network of subterranean tunnels, some of which lead directly eastward under the site of Dome of the Rock. Large areas underneath the Temple Mount are honeycombed with secret passages and huge cisterns, as reported by the Jewish historian Flavius Josephus.

Thirty-four cisterns were discovered that would have held a water supply lasting many months. The cisterns were cut out of the limestone underlying the Temple Mount, and combined they could hold more than twelve million gallons of water. Water storage was essential for the sanctuary services as well as for water reserves for the city's population in case of a prolonged siege. When the Muslims learned of this discovery, Islamic authorities demanded that the underground Western Gate be sealed, and the Israeli government agreed to limit the archaeological excavations.

Another confirmation of the location of the ancient Temple and Holy of Holies is the site of a small Arab cupola. It lies to the north of the Dome of the Rock and sits on an east-west line from the sealed Eastern Gate and the small, Arab, circular structure known as Qubbat al-Arwah (the Dome of the Spirits). It stands alone on a raised, flat, foundation stone composed of the original bedrock of Mount Moriah. The Arabs also call this site Qubbat al-Alouah (the Dome of the Tablets), and these two names may well reveal the ancient knowledge that this rock is the foundation stone that the Holy of Holies was built on. The Mishnah records that there was a foundation stone in the floor of the Holy of Holies known as Even Sheteyeh and that the ark of the covenant rested upon this foundation stone in Solomon's Temple. In the Second Temple, the Jewish Mishnah commentary records that the foundation stone stood alone in the Holy of Holies because the ark of the covenant was missing. The ark disappeared from the Temple at some point between Solomon's reign and the Babylonian invasion by Nebuchad-nezzar in 605 BC. The detailed biblical account of the Temple vessels captured by the Babylonian army does not list the ark of the covenant. Several top rabbis believe the ark is now back safely in Israel, where it remains hidden in secret until God gives the signal to rebuild the Temple. In my book *Armageddon,* I explore the strange history of the ark of the covenant's removal to Ethiopia three thousand years ago and its possible return to Israel at the end of the Ethiopian civil war in 1991.

In 1896, archaeologists discovered a cistern north of the Dome of the Rock, only a short distance southeast of the Dome of the Spirits, which conformed exactly to its description in the Jewish Mishnah. It was originally located between the Temple porch and the altar of sacrifice. This pit was designed to contain the libation offerings connected with the Temple worship services. The existence of this cistern helps confirm the location of the Holy of Holies in the Second Temple.

As this diagram of the Temple Mount illustrates, the Third Temple can be rebuilt on the exact location of Solomon's original Temple (and the Second Temple), with the Holy of Holies built around the ancient foundation stone that is now occupied by the Dome of the Spirits. This means the Third Temple can be rebuilt without disturbing the site of the Dome of the Rock. In addition, the pictures of the model of the Second Temple show that the Third Temple could be rebuilt on the original site, and the Dome of the Rock could remain in the Court of the Gentiles more than 150 feet to the south of the rebuilt Temple, as indicated in John's prophecy (see Revelation 11:1–2).

An Israeli group calling itself Netemanei Har Habayit, the Faithful of the Temple Mount, has created an accurate model of the Second Temple, and there is reliable information that a trust fund has been set up to pay the building costs. The Temple Mount is in Israeli hands, and the exact site for rebuilding is known. A Temple priesthood is in training by Rabbi Goren's yeshiva at Ateret Cohanim. The preconditions are coming together for the rebuilding of the Temple.

*This scale model of the Second Temple provides an accurate picture of what the Third Temple would look like if current plans for rebuilding move forward.*

## THE SANHEDRIN IS BEING RECONSTITUTED

One essential requirement for the rebuilding of the Temple is the reestablishment of the highest Jewish court of law—the Sanhedrin—which has not existed for sixteen centuries, since its last meeting in approximately 453 in Tiberias, Israel. On October 13, 2004, a group of seventy-one chosen rabbis received special rabbinic ordination according to the rules as specified by Moses Maimonides (AD 1200). Participants included numerous Orthodox religious leaders from across Israel, including the two former chief rabbis of Israel—Ovadiah Josef, former chief rabbi of the Sephardic Jews (Middle Eastern Jews), and Josef Elyashiv, the former chief rabbi of the Ashkenazi Jews (European Jews). Elyashiv is considered by many to be the spiritual heir of the biblical Moses and therefore spiritually in a position to ordain seventy other leaders required for a full Sanhedrin membership. The formal convening of the reconstituted Sanhedrin occurred January 20, 2005, in Jerusalem. Rabbi Yeshai Ba'avad stated, "The goal is to have one rabbinic body in Jerusalem that will convene monthly and issue rulings on central issues. This is the need of the generation and of the hour."[6]

Rabbis at the Sanhedrin convention discussed ideas related to building the Third Temple, including the construction of an altar on the Temple Mount that would be used for the Passover offering of a lamb during a future Passover. They also discussed Rabbi Ben-Yosef's concept of reinstating the Sanhedrin's religious authority to announce Rosh Hodesh, the sacred day that marks the beginning of each new lunar month. "It is very important to reinstate the Sanhedrin's authority to announce the month, because it will force people to understand that God gave us the power to control the calendar and our own destiny," according to Ben-Yosef, a leading member of the Sanhedrin.[7]

Rabbi Yisrael Ariel, a key Sanhedrin member, stated: "Whether this will be the actual Sanhedrin that we await, is a question of time—just like the establishment of the State; we rejoiced in it, but we are still awaiting something much more ideal."[8] It started in Tiberias but convened in Jerusalem in January 2005 and thereafter each month.

Additional Sanhedrin meetings were convened in Jerusalem to discuss the appropriate rules for the rebuilding of the Temple and the resumption of Temple worship. In June 2005 Rabbi Adin Steinsaltz was elected as the temporary president of the resurrected Sanhedrin.

The Israeli rabbinical council that initiated the reestablishment of the Sanhedrin court has called on all Jewish groups involved in research on the rebuilding of the Temple to submit detailed architectural plans in preparation for the reconstruction. Such actions are of special interest to Muslim religious authorities who are responsible for the administration of the Dome of the Rock and the Al-Aqsa Mosque on the Temple Mount.

Plans to build the Third Temple have extended to the practical call on volunteers and donors to contribute to pay for the materials for the new Temple. Requested contributions and assistance include "the gathering and preparation of prefabricated, disassembled portions to be stored and ready for rapid assembly, 'in the manner of King David.' "[9]

## PRIESTLY ARTIFACTS ARE
## BEING RECONSTRUCTED

Rabbi Yisrael Ariel, one of the Israeli paratroopers who liberated the Temple Mount in the Six-Day War, now heads the Temple Institute in Jerusalem. In the last two decades, the institute has meticulously constructed more than eighty worship implements required for the future Temple. These worship objects include the seven-branch golden menorah, the table of shewbread, and incense vessels. After years of detailed research, scholars from the Temple Institute and the Faithful of the Temple Mount announced they are ready to complete the breastplate of the high priest: "After much research, the twelve types of stones in the breastplate have been found, each of which has special characteristics."[10]

## The Oil of Anointing

The book of Exodus describes the detailed instructions that God gave Moses regarding the worship vessels to be used in the Tabernacle. In addition, the Lord commanded Moses to gather five special ingredients that would combine into the oil of anointing, which was to be used to anoint the Tabernacle, Aaron the high priest, and the sacred objects of worship. After being used over many centuries in the Tabernacle and later in the First and Second Temples, the oil of anointing disappeared when the Romans destroyed the Second Temple. One of the five ingredients of this sacred oil is described in the Bible as "sweet cinnamon." This rare and very expensive oil was treasured by royalty, including Cleopatra of Egypt.

When the Roman armies devastated the land of Israel in AD 70, the only two groves where sweet cinnamon oil was cultivated were destroyed. Without that key ingredient, it would be impossible to reconstitute the oil of anointing. This oil is needed not only to anoint the high priest and the Temple vessels but also to anoint the Messiah when He appears. Daniel, in his prophecy of the seventy weeks, predicted that the ushering in of the kingdom of God would include the anointing of "the most Holy," the long-awaited Messiah of Israel. The word *messiah* (*christos* in Greek) means "the anointed." It is important to note that Jesus of Nazareth was never anointed with the sacred oil of anointing during His life on earth.

Daniel wrote: "Seventy weeks are determined upon thy people and upon thy holy city, to finish the transgression, and to make an end of sins, and to make reconciliation for iniquity, and to bring in everlasting righteousness, and to seal up the vision and prophecy, and *to anoint the most Holy*" (Daniel 9:24, emphasis added). The problem is that, with the loss of one of the key ingredients, it would be impossible to reconstitute the sacred oil.

However, a remarkable manuscript from the Dead Sea Scrolls was discovered in 1952. Although all of the thousands of other Dead Sea Scrolls were made of papyrus or leather, one scroll was made of copper. This remarkable scroll contained a detailed list of sixty-four places where treasures of the Second Temple were buried by Essene priests to keep them out of the hands of the invading Roman soldiers. A rabbit warren of subterranean cisterns and tunnels beneath Jerusalem and the Temple Mount allowed the priests to remove the Temple treasury and its worship vessels for safekeeping. (Significantly, the records do not reveal that most of the Temple treasure was captured by the Roman army.)

Following the detailed topographical instructions found in the copper scroll, a group of archaeologists in 1988 discovered a cave in the Judean wilderness that contained a clay jar filled with congealed oil. It has been determined to be the long-lost *shemen afarsimon* (oil of anointing). This team from the Vendyl Jones Research Institutes, in consortium with Hebrew University, discovered the oil-filled jar buried in a pit in Cave 13 of the Dead Sea caves. The Talmud declares that a single drop of this special oil will turn water white, and this was confirmed by investigators. In addition, extensive testing by the Pharmaceutical Department of Hebrew University established that the oil dated from the first century.

The rediscovery of the oil of anointing and its possession by the two chief rabbis of Israel makes it possible for Daniel's prophecy of the anointing of the Messiah finally to be fulfilled. It is one of the most significant prophetic developments that points to the imminent coming of the Messiah.

### Ancient Blue Dye for the Garments of the High Priest

The Bible and the Mishnah describe the necessity of using a certain blue dye to color the robes of the high priest. This dye was produced from a rare mollusk in the Mediterranean Sea and was thought to be extinct. For many years Jewish scholars suggested that it was impossible to resume the ancient Temple worship without having a supply of the blue dye. However, in the late 1990s, Israeli divers discovered the rare mollusk, the hillazon snail *(Murex trunculus),* in the Red Sea. A thick liquid extracted from the gland of the mollusk produces the rich blue dye. The Temple Institute in Jerusalem created a supply of the dye, which was used in the creation of all the necessary garments required in Temple worship. The unspun wool for the robe is dipped into this liquid, which soon turns a bright green color. When the now-green wool is exposed to light, it turns a rich blue color. Once it dries, the wool is spun by craftsmen into a blue thread that is incorporated into the garments required for the high priest of the Temple. Several years ago the Temple Institute gave me some linen that was colored with the rare blue dye.

The fulfillment of the prophecies regarding the supernatural defeat of the Islamic-Russian armies in the War of Gog and Magog and the rebuilding of the Temple in Jerusalem will set the stage for the return of Jesus Christ. He will defeat the Antichrist and set up His kingdom on earth. In the next chapter, we will see that God has prophesied He will reconcile the Arabs and the Jews. The descendants of Isaac and Ishmael who have lived as bitter enemies finally will be able to live together in peace—in the millennial kingdom of Christ.

# PEACE BETWEEN
# ARABS AND JEWS

*How God Will Bring About a Final Reconciliation*

The most enduring dispute in human history, the age-old conflict between Arabs and Jews, will be reconciled in our generation. This bitter conflict has raged in the last century with terrorism and repeated wars resulting in the deaths of millions of innocent and not-so-innocent people throughout the Middle East. Finally the causes of this ancient hatred and fear will be removed from the hearts of all mankind, including Arabs and Jews.

When all the prophecies of the Word of God are fulfilled, the Messiah will return to establish the long-sought kingdom of God on earth. Peace and justice will prevail when Jesus rules from the throne of David. Jerusalem, which has known millenniums of violence and death, will finally know peace as indicated by its ancient name: Jer-u-salem, literally "city of peace." The name is ironic because no other city in history has been besieged and conquered more than Jerusalem. King David conquered the ancient city, which was then known as Jebus. Later, the Egyptians, Babylonians, Hasmoneans, Romans, Persians, Arabs, European Crusaders, Turks, and the British in turn conquered Jerusalem. At least twenty-seven times over the last four thousand years, Jerusalem has fallen to its enemies. The spectacular Six-Day War in 1967 witnessed the final conquest of Jerusalem by a Jewish army and the capture of the Temple Mount by Jews for the first time in almost two thousand years.

Following Christ's devastating defeat of the armies of the Antichrist and his two-hundred-million-man army of the "kings of the East" at the battle of Armageddon, He will cleanse the defiled Temple. Then Christ will commence His eternal reign as "Prince of Peace" in the eternal kingdom of God.

## THE ONGOING WAR ON TERROR

More than one hundred thousand trained terrorists are scattered throughout more than eighty nations. Many millions of Muslims, while not joining the war against the West, rejoiced when the terrorist attacks occurred on September 11, 2001, and when subsequent attacks occurred in Madrid, Bali, and London. Terrorist groups have dedicated themselves to the acquisition of nuclear, biological, and chemical weapons. If terrorists don't yet possess sufficient nuclear, biological, and chemical weapons to destroy key Western cities, it is only a matter of time. Those who love freedom and democracy must stay the course in the long-term war to destroy the Muslim terrorist groups before they succeed in destroying everyone who does not share their fundamentalist, militant views.

As Western nations and their allies around the world utilize their tremendous strengths—powerful political, economic, financial, intelligence, and military forces—we will prevail against our terrorist enemies. But it is crucial that we not lose sight of the spiritual dimension of this global crisis. We are not alone in the war on terror. Twenty-five centuries ago the prophet Isaiah reminded us that God is in total control of the events that are now unfolding. "All nations before him are as nothing; and they are counted to him less than nothing, and vanity" (Isaiah 40:17). Nothing can happen to your family, your city, and your nation unless Jesus Christ permits it.

Three thousand years ago King Solomon recorded God's promise to His people: "If my people, which are called by my name, shall humble themselves, and pray, and seek my face, and turn from their wicked ways; then will I hear from heaven, and will forgive their sin, and will heal their land" (2 Chronicles 7:14).

It is essential that those who love religious and political freedom pray that God will give our leaders the wisdom to understand this complex situation and make the right decisions in defense of the West. It would be easy to let the terror crisis overwhelm us, leading to inaction. But the apostle Paul declared, "For God hath not given us the spirit of fear; but of power, and of love, and of a sound mind" (2 Timothy 1:7). Those who have a personal faith in Jesus Christ can trust Him to give them "a sound mind" as they make spiritual and practical preparations to meet the unprecedented challenge to our freedom. King David declared his faith in the Lord to guide and provide for him in the face of danger: "The angel of the LORD encampeth round about them that fear him, and delivereth them. O taste and see that the LORD is good: blessed is the man that trusteth in him. O fear the LORD, ye his saints: for there is no want to them that fear him" (Psalm 34:7–9).

David's life was filled with disaster, challenges, and betrayals by family and associates, as well as tremendous victories over his enemies. David also taught us to trust in God's mercy and supernatural provision. He wrote about God's promise of His provision for those who place their faith and trust in Him. David wrote, "I have been young, and now am old; yet have I not seen the righteous forsaken, nor his seed begging bread" (Psalm 37:25).

## THE LORD'S ETERNAL PROVISION

Jesus Christ is the Son of God who sacrificed His life on the cross to pay the price for our sinful rebellion against God. If you have not trusted Christ as your personal Lord and Savior, you need to carefully consider this vital issue today. Every one of us must decide whom we will ultimately follow.

Either we will give our allegiance to the true God who is revealed in the Bible, or we will follow the false gods of this world.

Who will be the god of your life? Will you give your allegiance to Jesus Christ, or will you choose to worship yourself? Either you will admit you are a rebellious sinner in need of God's pardon and accept Jesus Christ as your Lord, or you will insist on remaining the god of your own life and pay the ultimate price: spending eternity in hell, separated from God.

The Word of God warns us that our spiritual pride is our first and greatest sin. Our sinful pride is expressed in the stubborn attitude of insisting on having our own way, even at the cost of experiencing an eternity without God. The great English poet John Milton wrote about this fundamental choice that confronts every one of us. In his epic poem *Paradise Lost,* Milton wrote that in the end, the choice of every unrepentant soul is described by these words: "Better to reign in Hell than serve in Heav'n."[1]

Your personal choice regarding your relationship to God will determine your eternal destiny. Ultimately, you must choose either heaven or hell. If you choose to ask God to forgive your sins and you commit your life to Jesus Christ, the Scriptures make it clear that you will meet Him as your Lord and Savior at the Resurrection. If you reject Jesus Christ's claim to be the Lord of your life, you have instead chosen to meet Him as your final Judge at the end of your life.

The apostle Paul prophesied God's final victory: "For it is written, As I live, saith the Lord, every knee shall bow to me, and every tongue shall confess to God" (Romans 14:11). Every one of us will finally bow our knees in acknowledgment of Christ's glory as Lord God. The only question is this: will you repent of your sinful rebellion against God and bow your knee today to Christ as your personal Lord and Savior, or will you reject His offer of salvation and be forced to finally bow to Him at the Last Day when you meet Him as your final Judge?

In light of the many prophetic signs that point to Christ's imminent return, each of us must make our choice. God warns us, "For all have sinned, and come short of the glory of God" (Romans 3:23). Every day, rebellion against God is leading men and women inexorably toward an eternity in hell without God. "For the wages of sin is death; but the gift of God is eternal life through Jesus Christ our Lord" (Romans 6:23).

But God loves every one of us so much that He sent His Son, Jesus Christ, to suffer the punishment that is due us because of our sins. Any person who will confess his sinful rebellion and ask for God's forgiveness will receive it. John, the beloved disciple, declared, "But as many as received him [Jesus], to them gave he power to become the sons of God, even to them that believe on his [Jesus'] name" (John 1:12).

The only basis by which we will be allowed to enter heaven will be our relationship to Jesus. It is impossible for a holy God to allow a sinner who rejects His forgiveness to enter heaven. Since we are all sinners, none of us can enter heaven on our own merits. So it was necessary that someone who was perfectly sinless take our place to pay the personal penalty of physical and spiritual death. The only one who could qualify as a perfect sacrifice was Jesus Christ, the holy, sinless Son of God.

Christ's sacrificial death on the cross paid the full price that we should have paid ourselves. If we accept God's offer of pardon for our sins, we will be able to stand before the judgment seat of God, saved by Christ's righteousness: "For he [God] hath made him [Jesus] to be sin for us, who knew no sin; that we might be made the righteousness of God in him" (2 Corinthians 5:21).

Jesus Christ's atoning death for our sins is perhaps the greatest mystery in creation. Jesus is the only person in history who, by His sinless life, was qualified to enter heaven. Yet He loved us so much that He chose to die on the cross to pay the price for our salvation. In a marvelous demonstration of God's mercy, the perfect righteousness of Jesus is credited to our personal accounts with God when we choose to repent of our sins and follow Him.

The Lord promises believers eternal life in heaven: "This is the will of him that sent me, that every one which seeth the Son, and believeth on him, may have everlasting life: and I will raise him up at the last day" (John 6:40). The moment you commit your life to Christ, you will receive eternal life. Though your body will someday die, He has promised that you will live forever with Christ in heaven if you place your full trust in Him. "For God so loved the world, that he gave his only begotten Son, that whosoever believeth in him should not perish, but have everlasting life" (John 3:16).

Nicodemus was a righteous religious leader in ancient Israel. After listening to Christ's teaching, he visited Jesus secretly one night and asked Him about the way of salvation. Jesus answered in these words, "Verily, verily, I say unto thee, Except a man be born again, he cannot see the kingdom of God" (John 3:3). It isn't enough that you intellectually accept the historical truth about Christ's death and resurrection. To be truly "born again," you must sincerely repent of your sinful life, asking Jesus to forgive you as you wholeheartedly place your faith and trust in Him. This decision will transform your life forever. God will give you a new purpose and meaning to your life.

Your decision to accept or reject Jesus Christ as your personal Savior is the most important decision you will ever make. However, deciding to accept His forgiveness and to follow Christ is only the beginning. Jesus commands His disciples, "Follow Me." Your commitment to Christ will transform your purposeless life into a new life filled with joy, peace, and spiritual purpose beyond anything you have ever known. Jesus challenges you to consider your choice in terms of eternity: "For what shall it profit a man, if he shall gain the whole world, and lose his own soul?" (Mark 8:36). Naturally, you will face many spiritual challenges after you accept Christ as your Lord and Savior, but God will never abandon you. Jesus promises to send you His Holy Spirit to empower you and give you comfort to face the spiritual challenges that lie ahead.

Jesus Christ is the promised Messiah who will return to earth to reign as king. If you have not submitted to him as the Lord of your life, why not confess your sins, ask for His forgiveness, and put your trust in Him right now?

# Appendix A

# THE PALESTINIAN
# CALL FOR JIHAD

Meeting in Cairo, Egypt, in June 1974, the Palestine National Council adopted the following political program.

> The Palestine National Council...resolves the following:
> 1. ...The Council...refuses...resolution [242]....
> 2. The Palestine Liberation Organization will employ all means, and first and foremost armed struggle, to liberate Palestinian territory and to establish the independent combatant national authority for the people over every part of Palestinian territory that is liberated.[1]

The official stance has not changed since 1974. An employee of the Palestinian Authority, Imam Sheikh Ibrahim Madhi, preached a Friday sermon at the Sheikh 'Ijlin Mosque in Gaza City that was broadcast live on April 12, 2002, by Palestinian Authority television. His statements not only reaffirmed the substance of the 1974 political program but also reaffirmed the cause of jihad against Israel:

> One of these days, we will enter Jerusalem as conquerors...and all of Palestine as conquerors....
> Anyone who does not attain martyrdom in these days should

wake in the middle of the night and say: "My God, why have
you deprived me of martyrdom for your sake?[2]

Beyond the official resolutions and formal statements of the PLO and
the Palestinian Authority (PA), there is the indoctrination of Palestinian
schoolchildren. In 2003, an inflammatory textbook titled *Islamic Culture*
was produced for eleventh-grade students by the PA's Ministry of Education. In spite of treaties and negotiations between the PA and Israel to pro-
hibit incitement to jihad and martyrdom, this textbook is only one of
many that psychologically prepare young Palestinians to assume the appro-
priateness of suicide martyrdom and other forms of violence against Jews.
The textbook declares:

Islam is Allah's religion for all human beings. It should be proclaimed and invite [people] to join it wisely and through appropriate preaching and friendly discussions. However, such
methods may encounter resistance and the preachers may be prevented from accomplishing their duty…then, Jihad and the use
of physical force against the enemies become inevitable…

Jihad is an Islamic term that equates to the term war in other
nations. The difference is that Jihad has noble goals and lofty
aims, and is carried out only for the sake of Allah and for His
glory."[3]

# Appendix B

# Plans for the New Sanhedrin

Christians are especially interested in plans being made in Israel to reconvene the ancient Sanhedrin. Following is a statement issued by the Israel Torah Foundation that summarizes the reasons behind reinstituting the Sanhedrin:

> For the prophecies to be fulfilled and the Temple rebuilt, the Nation must...leadership, political and spiritual, worthy of the honour....
>
> The SANHEDRIN is needed today...
> * to achieve the long-awaited redemption of the People and the Land;
> * to restore Torah law and Jurisprudence...;
> * to reunite the Hebrew Nation.[1]

# Appendix C

# DIRECT LINKS BETWEEN
# IRAQ AND AL QAEDA

The news media continue to question the existence of direct connections between Iraq and al Qaeda prior to the deposing of Saddam Hussein. Here is additional evidence that Hussein directly supported terrorism.

Among the senior al Qaeda operatives in Iraq prior to the war was Othman Suleiman Daoud, an Afghan national. Daoud was believed to be based in the Sunni Triangle north of Baghdad, the focus of the insurgency against the U.S. military. Another al Qaeda leader in Iraq was Faraj Shaabi, a Libyan national. Sources said Shaabi spent most of the years between 1990 and 2000 in Sudan until he was ordered by Osama bin Laden to transfer to Iraq. Meanwhile, in 2004, a sixteen-page, top-secret government memo to the U.S. Senate Intelligence Committee revealed that bin Laden and Saddam Hussein had an operational relationship from the early 1990s to 2003 that involved training in explosives and weapons of mass destruction as well as financial and logistical support. This relationship may have included the October 12, 2000, bombing of the USS *Cole* in Yemen and the September 11, 2001, attacks on the United States.

A memo dated October 27, 2003, was sent from Undersecretary of Defense for Policy Douglas J. Feith to Senators Pat Roberts and Jay Rockefeller, the chairman and vice-chairman, respectively, of the Senate Intelligence Committee. The memo was written in response to a request from the committee as part of its investigation into prewar intelligence claims made by the Bush administration. The memo cites reports from a variety of domestic and foreign spy agencies, including the FBI, the Defense Intelligence Agency, the National Security Agency, and the Central Intelligence Agency. Much of the evidence is detailed, conclusive, and corroborated by multiple sources. The memo reports that Hussein's willingness to help bin Laden plot an attack against Americans began in 1990, shortly before the first Gulf War, and continued through Hussein's overthrow.[1]

The memo states that bin Laden sent "emissaries to Jordan in 1990 to meet with Iraqi government officials." At some unspecified point in 1991, according to a CIA analysis, "Iraq sought Sudan's assistance to establish links to al-Qaeda."[2] The primary go-between throughout these early stages was Sudanese strongman Hassan al-Turabi, a leader of the al Qaeda–affiliated National Islamic Front.

A defector reported that "al-Turabi was instrumental in arranging the Iraqi–al Qaeda relationship." The defector said Iraq sought al Qaeda influence, through its connections with Afghanistan, to facilitate the shipment of proscribed weapons and equipment to Iraq, violating U.N. sanctions against Iraq. In return, Iraq provided al Qaeda with training and instructors. Another man, Mamdouh Mahmud Salim, who is described in the memo as bin Laden's "best friend," was involved in planning the simultaneous bombings in 1998 of the U.S. embassies in Kenya and Tanzania. According to the memo, the CIA believes "fragmentary evidence points to possible Iraqi involvement" in the bombing of the USS *Cole* in October 2000. Two members of al Qaeda were sent to Iraq following the attack on the *Cole,* the memo states, to be trained in weapons of mass destruction and to obtain information on "poisons and gases."[3]

And according to the CIA, in December 2000 the Saudi National Guard went on alert after learning Saddam Hussein had agreed to "assist al Qaeda in attacking U.S./U.K. interests in Saudi Arabia." More evidence of the Iraq–al Qaeda connection was found when Iraq was liberated after the U.S. invasion in 2003. Documents found in the bombed-out headquarters of the Mukhabarat, Iraq's secret police, show Hussein brought a bin Laden aide to Baghdad in early 1998 from bin Laden's former base in Sudan to arrange closer ties and to seek an in-person meeting. (Al Qaeda was based in Sudan until 1996, when its leadership moved to Afghanistan.) The paper trail indicates the meeting ended with arrangements being discussed for bin Laden to visit Baghdad. The documents do not make clear whether the meeting took place. The 1998 visit described in the documents occurred less than five months before bin Laden became a household name in the West, when Washington zeroed in on him after the bombings of two U.S. embassies in Africa later that year.[4]

Yusuf Galan, who was photographed being trained at a camp run by bin Laden, is now in jail in Madrid. The indictment against him, drawn up by investigating Spanish judge Baltasar Garzon, claims Galan was "directly involved with the preparation and carrying out of the attacks...by the suicide pilots on 11 September."[5] Evidence of Galan's links with Iraqi government officials came to light as investigators pored over more than forty thousand pages of documents seized in raids at the homes of Galan and seven alleged co-conspirators. It is worth noting that Richard Clarke, the former counterterrorism official who authored a book critical of the Bush administration and insisted Hussein had no connection to al Qaeda, believed in the link in 1999. He defended President Bill Clinton's attack on a Sudanese pharmaceutical plant by revealing the United States was "sure" it manufactured chemical warfare materials produced by Iraqi experts in cooperation with bin Laden.

Clarke told the *Washington Post* in a January 23, 1999, story that U.S. intelligence officials had obtained a soil sample from the El Shifa pharmaceutical plant in Khartoum, which was hit with Tomahawk cruise missiles in retaliation for bin Laden's role in the August 7, 1998, U.S. embassy bombings in Africa. The sample contained a precursor of VX nerve gas, which Clarke said would have become fully active VX nerve gas if mixed with bleach and water. Clarke told the *Washington Post* the United States did not know how much of the substance was produced at El Shifa or what happened to it. But he said that "intelligence exists linking bin Laden to El

Shifa's current and past operators, the Iraqi nerve gas experts and the National Islamic Front in Sudan," the *Post* reported.[6]

Clarke later changed his story. "There is absolutely no evidence that Iraq was supporting al-Qaeda ever," he stated.[7]

U.S. forces in Baghdad obtained documents that provide evidence of a direct link between Hussein's regime and the 9/11 attacks. Rosters of officers in the Fedayeen Saddam list Lt. Col. Ahmed Hikmat Shakir, who was present at the January 2000 al Qaeda summit in Kuala Lumpur, Malaysia, at which the 9/11 attacks were planned, the paper reported.[8]

The fedayeen was the elite paramilitary group run by Hussein's son Uday, which was deployed to do much of the regime's dirty work. The United States has never been sure if Shakir was at the Kuala Lumpur meeting on behalf of Hussein's regime or whether he was there on his own as an Iraqi Islamist. The *Wall Street Journal* cautioned that it is possible the Shakir listed on the rosters is not the Iraqi of the same name with proven al Qaeda connections. Reported accounts of the al Qaeda planning summit said Shakir had a job at the Kuala Lumpur airport he obtained through an Iraqi intelligence agent at the Iraqi embassy.

Among the al Qaeda operatives in attendance were the two who flew American Airlines Flight 77 into the Pentagon—Khalid al Midhar and Nawaz al Hamzi—and Ramzi bin al Shibh, the operational planner of the 9/11 attacks. Also in attendance was Tawfiz al Atash, a high-ranking bin Laden lieutenant and the mastermind of the USS *Cole* bombing. Shakir left Malaysia on January 13, 2000, four days after the summit finished, then turned up in Qatar, where he was arrested on September 17, 2001, just days after the attacks in New York and Washington DC.[9]

A search of Shakir's home uncovered phone numbers of the 1993 World Trade Center bombers' safe houses and contacts along with information related to a 1995 al Qaeda plot to blow up a dozen commercial airliners over the Pacific. But Shakir, inexplicably, was released after a brief detention, and he flew to Amman, Jordan, where he was arrested again. The Jordanians released him, however, with the mysterious approval of the

CIA, after pressure from the Iraqis and Amnesty International. He was last seen returning to Baghdad.

The information supports other journalists who have uncovered a connection between Iraq and al Qaeda, including Jayna Davis, author of *The Third Terrorist: The Middle East Connection to the Oklahoma City Bombing.* In her book, Davis suggests the 9/11 attacks possibly could have been prevented if evidence of an Iraqi and al Qaeda link to the bombing of the Alfred P. Murrah Federal Building in Oklahoma City had been pursued. Davis wrote that in November 1997, Hussain Hashem al-Hussaini—a former Iraqi Republican Guardsman whom multiple eyewitnesses identified as Timothy McVeigh's elusive accomplice, John Doe No. 2—confided to his psychiatrist that he was anxious about his airport job because "if something were to happen there, I [al-Hussaini] would be a suspect."[10]

At the time, al-Hussaini was employed at Boston's Logan International Airport, where two of the four 9/11 suicide hijackings originated.

Davis also reveals court records that suggest McVeigh's and Terry Nichols's accused Middle Eastern handlers had foreknowledge of the 9/11 plot. In addition, Davis discusses information she first uncovered in 1995 that Nichols learned the macabre genius of terrorist bomb making under the training of Philippines-based, al Qaeda explosives expert Ramzi Yousef, the convicted mastermind of the 1993 World Trade Center bombing.[11]

In February 2004, columnist and author Jonathan Schanzer met in a Kurdish prison with Abdul Rahman al-Shamari, who claims he worked for a man who was Hussein's envoy to al Qaeda. In the interview, al-Shamari confirmed he was involved in assisting Ansar al Islam, an al Qaeda affiliate responsible for attacks against Kurdish and Western targets in northern Iraq. Weapons, "mostly mortar rounds," were supplied to the terrorists, the prisoner told Schanzer. Besides weapons, al-Shamari says, Saddam's secret police, the Mukhabarat, helped the terror group financially "every month or two months."[12]

The terrorist group Ansar al-Islam operated openly in northern Iraq under the direction of Hussein's Iraqi Intelligence Service from September

2001 until the American invasion of Iraq in March 2003 destroyed its bases and killed or imprisoned most of its agents. In an article written for the Washington Institute for Near East Policy, titled "Ansar al-Islam: Iraq's al-Qaeda Connection," Schanzer wrote:

> In August 2001, leaders of several Kurdish Islamist factions reportedly visited the al-Qaeda leadership in Afghanistan with the goal of creating an alternate base for the organization in northern Iraq. Their intentions were echoed in a document found in an al-Qaeda guest house in Afghanistan vowing to "expel those Jews and Christians from Kurdistan and join the way of Jihad, [and] rule every piece of land...with the Islamic Shari'a rule." Soon thereafter, Ansar al-Islam was created using $300,000 to $600,000 in al-Qaeda seed money, in addition to funds from Saudi Arabia.[13]

In December 2003, it was reported that Iraqi officers interrogated by U.S. and coalition officials said Hussein, through Saudi contacts, had invited al Qaeda insurgents to form suicide and other units to stop the U.S. military in March 2003. Hussein's contacts with al Qaeda, the officers told interrogators, preceded the September 11 attacks. They said Saudi envoys arranged for al Qaeda insurgents to enter Iraq and begin training in camps around Baghdad. The al Qaeda insurgents were trained at two camps, Nahrawan and Salman Pak, under the supervision of the Fedayeen Saddam. Officers said the Salman Pak training included ways to hijack airplanes. Training was conducted under the supervision of an unidentified Iraqi general. They said many of the al Qaeda insurgents left Iraq after their training stint.[14]

# Appendix D

# A SAUDI COMPARES EXTREMIST ISLAMIC IDEOLOGY TO NAZISM

Saudi Arabian columnist Muhammad bin 'Abd al-Latif Aal al-Sheikh published several articles in the Saudi daily *Al-Jazirah* in which he attacked the Muslim extremist ideology of the Al-Salafiyya al-Jihadiyya movement. *Al-Salafiyya al-Jihadiyya* is a term used by Islamist terrorists who claim they are following in the footsteps of the prophet Muhammad's generation. Aal al-Sheikh wrote that the Al-Salafiyya al-Jihadiyya movement's ideology was similar to or even worse than the Nazi ideology, which killed millions in the 1930s and 1940s and nearly destroyed Europe.

Aal al-Sheikh wrote an article on July 10, 2005, titled "Both Jihadist Salafism and Nazism Are Based on Hatred and Physical Elimination of the Other." He wrote: "Putting an end to terrorism is only possible by putting an end to the ideology that plants it in our society. A security solution is not sufficient... He [al-Maqdisi] preaches...terrorism out of purely political motives... Al-Salafiyya al-Jihadiyya...should be dealt with exactly as the Europeans dealt with the Nazis."[1] (Aal al-Sheikh is criticizing the teachings of Abu Muhammad al-Maqdisi, the spiritual leader of the Jihadist Salafist movement in Jordan and teacher of the late al Qaeda leader Abu Musab al-Zarqawi.)

In another article, Aal al-Sheikh asked the question, "Why aren't we fighting the religious scholars, theoreticians, and preachers of terrorism like criminals, murderers, and robbers?" He wrote: "After the ruin, destruction, and bloodshed that Nazism brought upon mankind…the world arose to fight against this murderous ideology…to prevent this ideology from spreading anew. The question arises of why, in light of the similarity between these two ideologies, we haven't learned a lesson from this human experience?"[2]

# Notes

## Introduction

1. World War I casualties found at http://en.wikipedia.org/wiki/World_War_I/ Casualties. World War II casualties found at http://en.wikipedia.org/wiki/ List_of_World_War_II_casualties _by_country.

2. It is interesting and ironic that this anti-Western system of teaching is supported financially by Saudi Arabia, officially a U.S. ally.

3. Bassam Tibi, "War and Peace in Islam," in *The Ethics of War and Peace: Religious and Secular Perspectives,* ed. Terry Nardin (Princeton, NJ: Princeton University Press, 1996), 129–31.

4. Lawrence Auster, "The Centrality of Jihad in Islam," *FrontPage Magazine,* August 20, 2004, www.frontpagemag.com/Articles/Printable.asp?ID=14744.

5. C. Snouck Hurgronje, *Mohammedanism* (New York: Putnam, 1916), 59.

## Chapter 1: The Roots of Arab Muslim Hatred

1. It's interesting that this saying is found in the French novel *Dangerous Liaisons,* written in 1782.

2. Max I. Dimont, *Jews, God and History* (New York: New American Library, 1962), 390. The Copts are descendants of the Egyptians from the age of the Pharaohs. Those of Hamitic origins are descendants of Noah's son Ham who settled in parts of Africa and Canaan.

3. See Seymour M. Hersh, *The Samson Option: Israel's Nuclear Arsenal and American Foreign Policy* (New York: Random House, 1991), 45–46.

## Chapter 2: God Brings His People Back to the Holy Land

1. Wilhelm Schneemelcher, ed., *Apocalypse of Peter, New Testament Apocrypha* (Philadelphia: Westminster Press, 1964), 668–69.

2. David Ben-Gurion, quoted in "David Ben-Gurion—A Brief Biography and Quotes," October 23, 2001, www.palestineremembered.com/Acre/Famous-Zionist-Quotes/Story638.html.

3. Leonard Stein, *The Balfour Declaration* (London: Vallentine, Mitchell, 1961), 548.

4. Joan Peters, *From Time Immemorial: The Origins of the Arab-Jewish Conflict over Palestine* (New York: Harper and Row, 1984), 421.

5. Emir Faisal, "Letter to Felix Frankfurter," March 3, 1919, www.amislam.com/feisal.htm.

6. Peters, *From Time Immemorial,* 426.

7. On April 3, 1948, a radio broadcast by the Near East Arabic Radio referred to this call for Arabs to abandon their homes, farms, and businesses: "It must not be forgotten that the Arab Higher Committee encouraged the refugees to flee their homes in Jaffa, Haifa and Jerusalem, and that certain leaders…make political capital out of their miserable situation." This quote was cited in "The Palestinian Refugees," www.mideastweb.org/refugees1.htm. See also www.eretzyisroel.org/~jkatz/refugees2.html.

8. H. Maverik, "Arab Refugees Versus Jewish Refugees from Arab Countries," www.netanyahu.org/arrefverjewr.html. See also "Palestinian Refugees Invited to Leave in 1948," EretzYisroel.Org, www.eretzyisroel.org/~peters/index.html.

9. Joseph B. Schechtman, *The Arab Refugee Problem* (New York: Philosophical Library, 1952), 8–9.

10. Schechtman, *The Arab Refugee Problem,* 8–9.

11. A report to President Harry Truman in 1951 confirms: "Arab leaders summoned Arabs of Palestine to mass evacuation…as the documented facts reveal." See Dennis Merrill, ed., "The Documentary History of the Truman Presidency," Lexis Nexis, www.lexisnexis.com/academic/2upa/Aph/TrumanDocumentary.asp.

12. In 1959, Walter Pinner conducted a careful analysis and determined that the "genuine refugees" numbered about 430,000. See Pinner, *How Many Arab Refugees?* (London: MacGibbon and Kee, 1959), 15–19.

13. Peters, *From Time Immemorial,* 17–18.

14. UNRWA Annual Report of the Director, July 1951–June 1952.

15. King Hussein quoted at EretzYisroel.Org, www.eretzyisroel.org/~jkatz/refugees2.html.

## Chapter 3: Koranic Prophecies of Islam's Defeat

1. For more on this, see George Sale, *The Koran* (Philadelphia: J. W. Moore, 1850), 58.

## Chapter 4: The Warrior Prophet

1. Bernard Lewis, "The Roots of Muslim Rage," *Atlantic Monthly,* September 1990, 3.
2. Also spelled Abd-al-Muttalib.
3. Also spelled Abu Talib.
4. The Kaaba in Mecca is a huge, cube-shaped, stone structure that served as the center of pagan Arab worship for centuries before Muhammad removed the idols and claimed it for Islam.
5. Sahih al-Bukhari, vol. 1, hadith no. 24.
6. Five Pillars of Islam, http://en.wikipedia.org/wiki/Five_Pillars_of_Islam.

## Chapter 5: The Sixth Pillar of Islam—Jihad

1. See www.islamundressed.com/.
2. Michael Youssef, *America, Oil, & the Islamic Mind: The Real Crisis Is the Gulf Between Our Ways of Thinking* (Grand Rapids: Zondervan, 1991), 129.
3. Edward Gibbon, *The Decline and Fall of the Roman Empire,* vol. 2 (Chicago: Encyclopaedia Britannica, 1980), 288.
4. Friedrich von Schlegel, *Philosophy of History* (New York: AMS Press, 1973), 331. In addition, historian Thomas Arnold considered Martel's unexpected victory to be "among those signal deliverances which have affected for centuries the happiness of mankind" (Thomas Arnold, *History of the Later Roman Commonwealth,* vol. 2 [London: Bickers and Son, 1882], 317).
5. Edward Gibbon, the influential English historian, wrote the definitive history of the West in his classic *The Decline and Fall of the Roman Empire.* Here is how he described the advance of Islam toward Western Europe (Gibbon, *Decline and Fall,* 293):

> A victorious line of march had been prolonged above a thousand miles from the rock of Gibraltar to the banks of the Loire; the repetition of an equal space would have carried the Saracens to the confines of Poland and the Highlands of Scotland; the Rhine is not more impassable than the Nile or Euphrates, and the Arabian fleet might have sailed without a naval combat into the mouth of the Thames. Perhaps the interpretation of the Koran would now be taught in the schools of Oxford, and her pulpits might demonstrate to a circumcised people the sanctity and truth of the revelation of Mohammed.

6.  Bernard Lewis, "The Roots of Muslim Rage," *Atlantic Monthly*, September 1990, 3.

7.  "Shia and other non-Wahhabi Muslim community leaders estimate that eighty percent of American mosques out of a total ranging between an official estimate of 1,200 and an unofficial figure of 4,000 to 6,000 are under Wahhabi control," according to Jonathan Dowd-Gailey, "Research Islamism's Campus Club: The Muslim Students' Association," Campus Watch, *Middle East Quarterly*, Spring 2004, www.campus-watch.org/article/id/1180.

8.  "Ayatollah Khomeini," Iran Chamber Society, www.iranchamber.com/history/rkhomeini/ayatollah_khomeini.php.

9.  Milton Viorst, *In the Shadow of the Prophet: The Struggle for the Soul of Islam* (Boulder, CO: Westview Press, 2001).

10. Samuel Huntington, *The Clash of Civilizations and the Remaking of World Order* (New York: Simon and Schuster, 1996), 51.

11. Rachel Ehrenfeld and Alyssa Lappen, "Financial Jihad," Human Events Online, September 22, 2005, www.humaneventsonline.com/article.php?id=9235.

12. The Investigative Project on Terrorism, "Backgrounder on the Fiqh Council of North America and the Council on American-Islamic Relations," www.investigativeproject.org/FCNA-CAIR.html.

13. Steve Emerson, "The American Islamic Leaders' 'Fatwa' Is Bogus," http://counterterror.typepad.com/the_counterterrorism_blog/2005/07/the_american_is.html.

14. Lewis, "The Roots of Muslim Rage," 3.

15. Canadian Natural's Horizon Project, www.cnrl.com/horizon.

16. Nation Master, Oil Reserves by Country, www.nationmaster.com/graph-T/ ene_oil_res.

17. Doug Cameron, "US Developers See Hope in Abandoned Oil Wells," *Financial Times,* October 11, 2004. This article is archived at www.ft.com/. The print edition of Financial Times is archived at http://news.ft.com/siteservices/. The article also is posted at www.energybulletin.net/2494.html.

## Chapter 6: Osama bin Laden Declares War on the West

1. Ely Karmon, "Terrorism Against Jews by Radical Islamic Organizations and Groups," *The Washington Institute for Near East Policy Policywatch,* no. 347 (October 1998): 29.

2. Alan Travis, "Experts Back Startling Heroin Claims," *Guardian,* October 3, 2001, www.guardian.co.uk/afghanistan/story/0,,562258,00.html. Also posted at http://opioids.com/afghanistan/heroin.html.

3. Usamah Bin-Muhammad Bin-Ladin and others, "Text of Fatwah Urging Jihad Against Americans," first published in Arabic in *Al-Quds al-'Arabi,* February 23, 1998. The English-language version was found at the Institute for Counter-Terrorism Web site, www.ict.org.il/articles/fatwah.htm. For the Arabic-language version, see www.alquds.co.uk/.

4. Usamah Bin-Muhammad Bin-Laden, "Declaration of War Against the Americans Occupying the Land of the Two Holy Places," issued August 23, 1996. First published in *Al-Quds al-'Arabi.* For the English-language translation, see http://cc .msnscache.com/cache.aspx?q=3272048407478&lang=en-US&mkt=en-US &FORM=CVRE. Also posted at www.kimsoft.com/2001/binladenwar.htm. For the Arabic-language version, see www.alquds.co.uk.

5. After the simultaneous terrorist bombings at the American embassies in Nairobi, Kenya, and Dar-es-Salam, Somalia, on August 7, 1998 (killing several hundred and wounding more than five thousand), the Sudanese government responded to pressure from the United States and expelled al Qaeda terrorists from the country.

6. Osama bin Laden, interview by John Miller, *Frontline,* PBS, May 1998, www.pbs.org/wgbh/pages/frontline/shows/binladen/who/interview.html.

7. Bin-Ladin and others, "Text of Fatwa Urging Jihad Against Americans."

8. See Yoram Schweitzer, "Osama Bin Ladin: Wealth Plus Extremism Equals Terrorism," July 27, 1998, Institute for Counter-Terrorism, www.ict.org.il/articles/articledet.cfm?articleid=40.

9. "Saudi Diplomat: Osama Bin Laden, Not Taliban, Real Power in Afghanistan," *Tampa Tribune,* October 5, 2001, http://multimedia.belointeractive.com/attack/middleeast/1005saudibl.html.

10. Zionist Organization of America's Israel News Connection, "Where's Osama? (A New Name and Face?)" http://geocities.com/zincisrael/features/f74Wheres_Osama.htm.

11. Bin-Ladin and others, "Text of Fatwa Urging Jihad Against Americans."

## Chapter 7: Al Qaeda's Strategies and Resources

1. Philip Webster and Roland Watson, "Bin Laden's Nuclear Threat," *London Times,* October 26, 2001.

2. Duncan Long, *The Bio-Terrorism Manual* (Plantation, FL: Life and Health Research Group, 2003), www.rense.com/bioter/bioterror.htm.

3. Long, *The Bio-Terrorism Manual.* See also "America's Foes Prepare to Wage Biological War Against U.S.," the International Business Center, www.financialprivacy.com/articles/preparedness_dep.htm.

4. "Hearing on U.S. Federal Efforts to Combat Terrorism," May 9, 2001, www.usdoj.gov/ag/testimony/2001/ag_statement_05_09_01.htm.

5. "U.S. Intelligence Consensus: Iraqi WMD Shipped to Syria," *World Tribune,* October 30, 2003, www.worldtribune.com/worldtribune/WTARC/2003/ss_syria_10_29.html/. Also posted at www.ualm.org.au/Syria_Files.asp?display=content&id=61.

6. Kenneth Timmerman, "Ex-Pentagon Official Says Russia Moved Saddam's WMDs," NewsMax, February 19, 2006, www.worldthreats.com/middle_east/ex-Pentagon.htm.

7. For more on this, see Georges Sada, *Saddam's Secrets* (Nashville: Integrity Publishers, 2006).

8. "Lab Tests Could Link Saddam's Missing WMDs to Jordan Plot,"

NewsMax.com, April 20, 2004, www.newsmax.com/archives/ic/2004/4/20/234509.shtml.

9. In spite of compelling evidence that al Qaeda terrorists acquired WMD from Iraq, the Western news media refused to acknowledge the link. For the most part, the media held firm in their contention that President Bush lied when he claimed Iraq had possessed WMD, including VX nerve gas, just before the invasion of Iraq. Almost without exception, the Western news media refused to identify the VX nerve gas that was to be used in the 2004 attack on Amman. Instead, the attempted VX attack was referred to as a "chemical weapon" attack. See, as just one example, "Al-Qaeda Planned Chemical Bomb Attack (Jordan)," www.free republic.com/focus/f-news/1120819/posts, April 19, 2004.

10. "Lab Tests Could Link Saddam's Missing WMDs to Jordan Plot." See also "Jordanian Authorities Foil Mega-Terror Attack," April 17, 2004, www.ict.org.il/spotlight/det.cfm?id=974.

11. Paul L. Williams, *Osama's Revenge: The Next 9/11: What the Media and the Government Haven't Told You* (Amherst, NY: Prometheus Books, 2004), 158.

12. Chidanand Rajghatta, "America Wakes Up to Osama's Nuke Dreams," *Times of India,* October 27, 2001, www1.timesofindia.indiatimes.com/cms.dll/articles how?art_id=1862859664.

13. Webster and Watson, "Bin Laden's Nuclear Threat," 3. See also Tony Wesolowsky, "Afghanistan: Nuclear Terrorism Poses Questionable Threat," *RFE/RL Weekday Magazine,* October 19, 2001, www.ransac.org/Projects%20and%20Publications/News/Nuclear%20News/2001/10_25_01.html#3c.

14. "Scores of Nuclear Devices Are Missing, Lebed Told Congress," *Russia Reform Monitor,* no. 314, September 18, 1997, American Foreign Policy Council, Washington DC, www.afpc.org/rrm/rrm314.htm.

15. William Potter, " 'The Peacemaker' Is a Warning to All," *Los Angeles Times,* September 29, 1997, sec. Metro.

16. "Nuclear Terrorism and Countermeasures," 1998 Congressional Hearings, Special Weapons: Nuclear, Chemical, Biological and Missile, October 1, 1997, transcript of testimony, www.fas.org/spp/starwars/congress/1997_h/has274010 _1.htm.

17. Yossef Bodansky, *Bin Laden: The Man Who Declared War on America* (New York: Random House, 2001), 328–30.

18. Scott Parrish, "Russia: Are Suitcase Nukes on the Loose? The Story Behind the Controversy," NTI, Center for Nonproliferation Studies, www.nti.org/db/ nisprofs/over/lebedlg.htm and http://cns.miis.edu/pubs/reports/lebedig.htm.

19. Bodansky, *Bin Laden,* 329–30. Additional indications of a sale of suitcase nuclear weapons is contained in a book by Andrew Cockburn and Leslie Cockburn, who claim that Chechen rebels warned the U.S. government in mid-1994 that they had acquired two tactical nuclear weapons. Chechen terrorist leaders warned they would transfer these weapons to Arab governments if the United States refused to recognize the independence of Chechnya from Russia. There are reports that the Chechen Muslim rebels gave U.S. intelligence enough technical information to convince them that they did, in fact, possess these deadly weapons. Apparently the Chechen rebels realized that Russia would retaliate with nuclear missiles if they dared to use the suitcase nuclear devices against Russia. Therefore, they decided to sell them to al Qaeda, which could more easily use such weapons because they do not represent a nation-state that could be subject to political or military retaliation. A secret intelligence group visited Chechnya but failed to verify this information. However, this report confirms that American intelligence agencies are concerned about a "terrorist nuclear bomb" (Andrew Cockburn and Leslie Cockburn, *One Point Safe* [New York: Doubleday, 1997], 101–3).

20. Richard Sale, "Israel Finds Radiological Backpack Bomb," United Press International, October 26, 2001, www.freerepublic.com/focus/fr/557120/posts.

21. The U.S. government expert who spoke to UPI's Richard Sale indicated that the weapon carried by the terrorist was a backpack device that Russian intelligence agents warned the CIA about in 1995 (Sale, "Israel Finds Radiological Backpack Bomb").

22. Williams, *Osama's Revenge,* 44–45.

23. Williams, *Osama's Revenge,* 157–58.

24. Williams, *Osama's Revenge,* 129.

25. Williams, *Osama's Revenge,* 88–89.

26. "70,000 'Cruise' Missiles—CIA Assessment," *Eye Spy* magazine, no. 12 (2002): 5.

27. Jack Kelly, "Terror Groups Hide Behind Web Encryption," *USA Today,* February 7, 2001, 1.

28. Nathan C. Masters, "Grad Student Gives al-Qaeda Bombing Map," *NewsMax* magazine, September 2003, 11. See also Laura Blumenfeld, "Dissertation Could Be Security Threat," *Washington Post,* July 8, 2003, sec. A, 1.

29. Masters, "Grad Student Gives al-Qaeda Bombing Map," 11.

30. "Al-Qaeda Uses Internet to Train Terrorists in Iraq: Report," *The Hindu,* August 7, 2005, www.hindu.com/thehindu/holnus/003200508071010.htm.

## Chapter 8: Islam's War Against All Perceived Enemies

1. "Expressions of Anti-Semitism in the Arab Press," Jewish Virtual Library, May 2001, www.jewishvirtuallibrary.org/jsource/anti-semitism/arabpress0501.html.

2. Shaker al-Nabulsi, "Terrorism in the Arab World Has Been Encouraged by Islamic Legal Scholars," *Al-Siyasa* (Kuwait), August 7, 2005. English translation by the Middle East Media Research Institute, Special Dispatch Series, no. 965, August 22, 2005, http://memri.org/bin/articles.cgi?Page=archives&Area=sd &ID=SP96505.

3. From Jihad Watch, www.jihadwatch.org/archives/007303.php.

4. Nimrod Raphaeli, " 'The Sheikh of the Slaughterers': Abu Mus'ab Al-Zarqawi and the Al-Qa'ida Connection," the Middle East Media Research Institute, July 1, 2005, no. 231, http://memri.org/bin/articles.cgi?Page=archives&area=ia &ID=IA23105.

5. Sheikh Muhammad Ali, interviewed August 19, 2005, on Hezbollah's Al-Manar television. English translation by the Middle East Media Research Institute, TV Monitor Project, clip no. 820, August 19, 2005, www.memritv.org/Transcript .asp?P1=820.

6. Cited by Moshe Sharon, "The Agenda of Islam—A War Between Civilizations," FaithFreedom.org, www.faithfreedom.org/Articles/MosheSharon40214%20.htm.

7. Robert S. Leiken, "Europe's Angry Muslims," *Foreign Affairs,* July–August 2005.

8. Daniel Pipes and Khalid Durn, "Muslim Immigrants in the United States," Center for Immigration Studies, August 2002, www.cis.org/articles/2002/ back802.html.

9. David B. Barrett, *World Christian Encyclopedia,* 2nd ed. (Oxford, England: Oxford University Press, 2001), 1:3.

10. Barrett, *World Christian Encyclopedia,* 1:5, table 1-2.

11. Lausanne Statistics Task Force on Evangelism, www.adherents.com/index .html.

12. Barrett, *World Christian Encyclopedia,* 1:13–14, table 1-4.

## Chapter 9: Iraq's Terror Connection

1. Ravi Nessman, "Marines Capture Camp Suspected as Iraqi Training Base for Terrorists," Associated Press, April 6, 2003.

2. "Gunning for Saddam," *Frontline,* PBS, November 8, 2001, www.pbs.org/wgbh/ pages/frontline/shows/gunning/interviews/khodada.html.

3. Hynek Kmonicek, Czech Ambassador to the United Nations, to James Beasley Jr., who filed a wrongful death suit against Saddam Hussein after 9/11, February 24, 2003.

4. Con Coughlin, "Documents Link Baghdad to 9/11," *Toronto National Post,* December 15, 2003, sec. A, 11.

5. Nidal died in 2002. Arab intelligence sources dispute the official Iraqi version of his death, which maintains that he committed suicide after his arrest by Iraqi agents. He was found shot numerous times in the chest with an AK47 rifle. Intelligence sources said Nidal was killed by Iraqi agents in his Baghdad office several days before his death was reported on August 19, 2002. See "Day of Infamy 2001, Memo: 9-11 Chief Trained by Saddam, Atta in Baghdad Under Abu Nidal's Tutelage Just Before Attacks" and Coughlin, "Documents Link Baghdad to 9/11," 11.

6. Coughlin, "Documents Link Baghdad to 9/11," 11.

7. "Iraqis Vote Osama bin Laden Man of 2001," *The Namibian,* January 14, 2002, www.namibian.com.na/2002/January/world/0238E53CC6.html.

8. National Commission on Terrorist Attacks upon the United States, *The 9/11 Commission Report: Final Report of the National Commission on Terrorist Attacks upon the United States* (Washington DC: U.S. Government Printing Office, 2004), 172, see www.gpoaccess.gov/911/index.html.

9. "Transcript: President Bush Speaks About 9/11 Commission," WashingtonPost .com, June 17, 2004, www.washingtonpost.com/wp-dyn/articles/A49013-2004 Jun17.html.

10. See Yossef Bodansky, *Bin Laden: The Man Who Declared War on America* (New York: Random House, 2001), 380–83.

11. Joseph Farah, "Osama-Saddam Links 9-11 Commission Missed," WorldNetDaily .com, June 18, 2004, www.worldnetdaily.com/news/article.asp?ARTICLE _ID=39025.

12. Larry Kudlow, "Target: Safe Harbor," National Review Online, September 6, 2002, www.nationalreview.com/kudlow/kudlow090602.asp.

13. Kudlow, "Target: Safe Harbor."

14. Laurie Mylroie, *The War Against America: Saddam Hussein and the World Trade Center Attacks: A Study of Revenge,* 2nd rev ed. (New York: Regan Books, 2001), 202–04.

15. Farah, "Osama-Saddam Links 9-11 Commission Missed."

16. Farah, "Osama-Saddam Links 9-11 Commission Missed."

17. Laurie Mylroie, *Study of Revenge: Saddam Hussein's Unfinished War Against America* (Washington DC: AEI Press, 2000), 255.

## *Chapter 10: The Deeper Threat of Terrorism*

1. Hafez al-Barghouti, "Let Us Revolt," editorial, *Al hayat al Jadida,* November 30, 1997.

2. Timothy Noah, "The PLO Rx: Give Blood, Threaten Cameramen, Call Me in the Morning," September 13, 2001, www.slate.com/id/1008286/.

3. Mark A. Moorstein, *Frameworks: Conflict in Balance* (New York: iUniverse, 2004), 248.

4. Chris Wattie, "CBC Stands by Its Ban on 'Terrorism' and 'Terrorist,'" *National Post,* July 19, 2005, sec. A, 16, www.cbcwatch.ca/?q=node/view/1177.

5. Wattie, "CBC Stands by Its Ban on 'Terrorism' and 'Terrorist,'" 16.

6. Daniel Pipes, "They're Terrorists—Not Activists or Victims," Jewish World Review, September 7, 2004, www.jewishworldreview.com/0904/pipes2004 _09_07.php3?printer_friendly.

7. *United States v. Enaam M. Arnaout,* 02 CR 892, "Government's Evidentiary Proffer Supporting the Admissibility of Coconspirator Statements," (N.D. Ill.), http://fl1 .findlaw.com/news.findlaw.com/hdocs/docs/ bif/usarnaout10603prof.pdf.

8. Elie Shuman, "What Makes Suicide Bombers Tick," June 4, 2001, www .habonimdror.org/resources/arab%20israeli%20conflict/peulot.htm.

9. *Yediot Aharonot,* September 3, 1995.

10. Shuman, "What Makes Suicide Bombers Tick."

11. Shuman, "What Makes Suicide Bombers Tick."

## Chapter 11: The Arab War Against Israel

1. The original article by Louis Rene Beres was published in the *New York Times,* May 16, 1948, translated by *The Peace Encyclopedia: The War of Independence, 1948,* Yahoodi Communications 2002, www.yahoodi.com/peace/warindep.html.

2. "Palestine as an Arab Ethnic Group Is a Modern Political Creation Since 1967," *Akhbar al-Yom,* October 11, 1947, EretzYisroel.Org, www.eretzyisroel.org/~jkatz/ creation.html.

3. Mitchell Bard, "The Palestinian Refugees," *Al-Misri,* October 11, 1949, www.jewishvirtuallibrary.org/jsource/History/refugees.html.

4. D. H. Miller, "Minutes of the Supreme Council," in *My Diary at the Conference of Paris,* 22 vols. (New York: Appeal Printing Co., 1924), 14:405.

5. Bernard Lewis, "The Palestinians and the PLO, a Historical Approach," *Commentary,* January 1975, 32–48.

6. *Palestine Royal Commission Report* (Geneva: League of Nations Publications, 1937), chap. 1, p. 6, para. 11.

7. "Grand Mufti Plotted to Do Away with All Jews in Mideast," *Response,* Fall 1991, 2–3, cited by Mitchell Bard, "The Mufti and the Führer," www.jewish virtuallibrary.org/jsource/History/muftihit.html.

8. "The PLO's Phased Plan," PalestineFacts.org, www.palestinefacts.org/pf_1967 to1991_plo_phasedplan_1974.php.

9. Following the announcement of the historic 1993 Israel-PLO agreement, PLO chairman Yasser Arafat announced that the Oslo Agreement "will be a basis for an independent Palestinian state in accordance with the Palestine National Coun-

cil resolution issued in 1974.... [The resolution] calls for the establishment of a national authority on any part of Palestinian soil from which Israel withdraws or which is liberated." (Arafat's announcement was broadcast on Radio Monte Carlo, September 1, 1993. It was cited in "Looking Back," DAFKA-News, www.dafka.org/NewsGen.asp?S=4&PageID=664.)

10. Shafiq Ahmad Ali, "Faysal Al-Husseini in His Last Interview: The Oslo Accords Were a Trojan Horse; The Strategic Goal Is the Liberation of Palestine from the [Jordan] River to the [Mediterranean] Sea," *Al-'Arabi,* June 24, 2001. English translation by the Middle East Media Research Institute, Special Dispatch Series, no. 236, July 2, 2001, www.memri.org/bin/articles.cgi?Page=archives &Area=sd&ID=SP23601.

11. *Jihad in America,* Steve Emerson, producer and director, PBSN-Heritage Foundation TV documentary, first broadcast November 21, 1994.

12. From the school textbook *Islamic Culture* (for eleventh grade), issued by the Palestinian Authority Ministry of Education and approved by the Jordanian Ministry of Education, 2003, 208. English translation by the Middle East Media Research Institute. For more on this, see "2003 Palestinian Authority Textbook Calls for Jihad and Martyrdom," *Special Report no. 22,* November 14, 2003, www.memri.org/bin/articles.cgi?Area=sr&ID=SR2203.

13.  Usama bin Muhammad bin in Laden, "Declaration of the World Islamic Front for Jihad Against the Jews and Crusaders," *Al-Quds al-'Arabi,* February 23, 1998, 3. For the Arabic language version, see www.alquds.co.uk.

## *Chapter 12: Will This War Signal the Last Days?*

1. Meir Z. Iotowitz, trans., *Bereishis—Genesis: A New Translation with a Commentary Anthologized from Talmudic, Midrashic and Rabbinic Sources* (New York: Mesorah Publications, 1980), 311.

2. Iotowitz, *Bereishis—Genesis,* 311.

3. J. H. Hertz, ed., *The Pentateuch and Haftorahs* (London: Soncino Press, 1961), 35.

4. *Yechezkel: The Book of Ezekiel/A New Translation with a Commentary Anthologized from Talmudic, Midrashic, and Rabbinic Sources* (New York: Mesorah Publications, 1980), 580–1.

5. Flavius Josephus, *Antiquities of the Jews,* in *The Works of Flavius Josephus,* trans. William Whiston (Grand Rapids: Kregel, 1960), 30.

6. Robert Young, *Analytical Concordance of the Holy Bible* (London: United Society for Christian Literature, 1971), 424, 627.

7. Arno C. Gaebelein, *The Prophet Ezekiel: An Analytical Exposition* (Neptune, NJ: Loizeaux Brothers, 1972), 257.

8. In Yerushalmi, Shabbat 1:3, the rabbis describe Elijah's preparing the hearts of the Jews prior to Magog's invasion of Israel (Babylonian Talmud, *Abodah Zarah* 3b [London: Soncino Press, 1935], 8–9).

9. *Yechezkel,* 581, citing *Chevlei Mashiach BiZemaneinu,* 134.

## Chapter 13: A New Temple for the Last Days

1. Following Israel's recapture of the Temple Mount during the Six-Day War, *Time* magazine published an article with the headline "Should the Temple Be Rebuilt?" The writer asked, "Has the time now come for the erection of the third Temple? Some Jews see plausible theological grounds for discussing reconstruction...Israel has already entered its 'Messianic Era.'" See Israel Eldad, "Should the Temple Be Rebuilt?" *Time* archive, June 30, 1967, www.time.com/time/archive/preview/0,10987,837052,00.html.

2. Moses Maimonides, *Hilchos Bais HaBechirah* in *Mishneh Torah,* trans. Eliyahu Touger (New York: Maznaim Publishing, 1986), 1.

3. Maimonides, *Mishneh Torah,* from the translator's introduction.

4. In March 1985, the television news magazine *60 Minutes* in a segment called "One Step in Heaven" reported that rabbinical students in Jerusalem were studying the reintroduction of the ancient Jewish rites of animal sacrifice. Less than five hundred yards to the northwest of Wilson's Arch, adjoining the Western Wall of the ancient Temple, I visited this yeshiva, or Jewish theological college, which was led by Rabbi Schlomo Goren, the former chief rabbi of the Israel Defense Forces. This is the same rabbi who blew the *shofar,* the ram's horn, immediately after the recapture of the Western Wall of the Temple in June 1967. In a *Newsweek* interview in November 1981, Goren declared that "the

secret of the location of the Ark will be revealed just prior to building the Third Temple." (See "New 'Sanhedrin' Plans Rebuilding of Temple: Israeli Rabbinical Body Calls for Architectural Blueprint," WorldNetDaily.com, June 8, 2005, www.worldnetdaily.com/news/article.asp?ARTICLE_ID =44672.)

5. Eldad, "Should the Temple Be Rebuilt?"

6. "Sanhedrin Launched in Tiberias," IsraelNationalNews.com, January 20, 2005, www.israelnationalnews.com/news.php3?id=70349.

7. Yaakov Katz, "Hear Ye, Hear Ye: 'Sanhedrin' Seeks David's Scion to Be King," *Jerusalem Post Online Edition,* January 12, 2005, News section, http://pqasb .pqarchiver.com/jpost/access/777670431.html?dids=777670431:777670431 &FMT=ABS&F.

8. "Sanhedrin Launched in Tiberias."

9. "New 'Sanhedrin' Plans Rebuilding of Temple."

10. "The Breastplate and Ephod of the High Priest—An Important Part of Worship in the Temple," *Temple Mount Faithful Newsletter,* Summer 2001, www.temple mountfaithful.org/Newsletters/2001/5761-9.htm.

## Chapter 14: Peace Between Arabs and Jews

1. John Milton, *Paradise Lost,* bk. 1, line 263.

## Appendix A: The Palestinian Call for Jihad

1. "The PNC Program of 1974," June 8, 1974, MidEast Web GateWay, www.mideastweb.org/plo1974.htm.

2. "Friday Sermon on Palestinian Authority TV," broadcast live on Palestine television, April 12, 2002. English translation by the Middle East Media Research Institute, Special Dispatch Series, no. 370, April 17, 2002, http://memri.org/bin/ articles.cgi?Page=archives&Area=sd&ID=SP37002.

3. *Islamic Culture for Eleventh Grade,* issued by the Palestinian Authority Ministry of Education and approved by the Jordanian Ministry of Education, 2003. English translation by the Middle East Media Research Institute.

## Appendix B: Plans for the New Sanhedrin

1. Taken from *The Sanhedrin of the Sixth Millenium*, pamphlet no. 58-007-740-2 published by the Israel Torah Foundation (ITF).

## Appendix C: Direct Links Between Iraq and al Qaeda

1. Stephen F. Hayes, "Case Closed: The U.S. Government's Secret Memo Detailing Cooperation Between Saddam Hussein and Osama bin Laden," *The Weekly Standard*, November 24, 2003, www.weeklystandard.com/Content/Public/Articles/000/000/003/378fmxyz.asp.

2. Hayes, "Case Closed."

3. Hayes, "Case Closed."

4. Joseph Farah, "Osama-Saddam Links 9-11 Commission Missed," WorldNetDaily .com, June 18, 2004, www.worldnetdaily.com/news/article.asp?ARTICLE _ID=39025.

5. Farah, "Osama-Saddam Links 9-11 Commission Missed."

6. Jim Curtis, "Iraq Conspired with Bin Laden to Produce WMDs...According to Richard Clarke," *Washington Post*, January 23, 1999, sec. A, 2.

7. Deroy Murduck, "Clarke's Not Blind," National Review Online, March 26, 2004, www.nationalreview.com/murdock/murdock200403260858.asp.

8. Farah, "Osama-Saddam Links 9-11 Commission Missed."

9. Ryan Mauro, *Death to America* (Baltimore: Publish America, 2005), 73–74.

10. Jayna Davis, *The Third Terrorist: The Middle East Connection to the Oklahoma City Bombing* (Nashville: Nelson, 2004), 211.

11. Davis, *The Third Terrorist*, 242.

12. Jonathan Schanzer, "Saddam's Ambassador to al Qaeda," *Weekly Standard*, March 1, 2004, vol. 009, no. 24, www.weeklystandard.com/Content/Public/Articles/000/000/003/768rwsbj.asp.

13. Jonathan Schanzer, "Ansar al-Islam: Iraq's Al-Qaeda Connection," Washington Institute for Near East Policy, PolicyWatch #699, January 15, 2003, www .washingtoninstitute.org/templateC05.php?CID=1577.

14. "More Damning Documents on Saddam," *Investors Business Daily, Inc.,*
    Investors.com, April 7, 2006, www.investors.com/editorial/IBDArticles.asp?
    artsec=20&artnum=1&issue=20060407.

## *Appendix D: A Saudi Compares Extremist Islamic Ideology to Nazism*

1. Muhammad bin 'Abd al-Latif Aal al-Sheikh, "Both Jihadist Salafism and Nazism Are Based on Hatred and Physical Elimination of the Other," *Al-Jazirah* (Saudi Arabia), July 10, 2005, quoted in "Saudi Columnist: Jihadist Salafist Ideology Is Like Nazism," Middle East Media Research Institute, Special Dispatch Series, no. 1007, October 17, 2005, http://memri.org/bin/articles.cgi?Page=archives &Area=sd&ID=SP100705/.

2. Muhammad bin 'Abd al-Latif Aal al-Sheikh, "Why Aren't We Fighting the Religious Scholars, Theoreticians, and Preachers of Terrorism like Criminals, Murderers, and Robbers?" *Al-Jazirah* (Saudi Arabia), quoted in "Saudi Columnist: Jihadist Salafist Ideology Is Like Nazism," Middle East Media Research Institute, Special Dispatch Series, no. 1007, October 17, 2005, http://memri .org/bin/articles.cgi?Page=archives&Area=sd&ID=SP100705.

# Selected Bibliography

Aburish, Saïd K. *Arafat: From Defender to Dictator.* London: Bloomsbury Publishing, 1998.

———. *Saddam Hussein: The Politics of Revenge.* New York: Bloomsbury Publishing, 2000.

Adams, James. *Secret Armies: Inside the American, Soviet, and European Special Forces.* London: Pan Books, 1988.

———. *The Next World War: Computers Are the Weapons and the Front Line Is Everywhere.* New York: Simon and Schuster, 1998.

Alexander, Yonah, and Michael S. Swetnam. *Usama bin Laden's al-Qaida: Profile of a Terrorist Network.* Ardsley, NY: Transnational Publishing, 2001.

Algosaibi, Ghazi A. *The Gulf Crisis.* London: Kegan Paul International, 1993.

Baxter, Jenny, and Malcolm Downing, eds. *The Day That Shook the World.* London: BBC, 2001.

Bennett, Ramon. *Philistine.* Keno, OR: Shekinah Books, 1995.

Bodansky, Yossef. *Bin Laden: The Man Who Declared War on America.* Roseville, CA: Prima Publishing, 2001.

———. *Islamic Anti-Semitism as a Political Instrument.* Houston: Freeman Center for Strategic Studies, 1999.

Bostom, Andrew G., ed. *The Legacy of Jihad: Islamic Holy War and the Fate of Non-Muslims.* Amherst, NY: Prometheus Books, 2005.

Brown, Rebecca. *Prepare for War.* New Kensington, PA: Whitaker House, 1992.

Coughlin, Con. *A Golden Basin Full of Scorpions: The Quest for Modern Jerusalem.* London: Little, Brown and Company, 1997.

———. *Saddam: King of Terror.* New York: Ecco, 2002.

Darwish, Adel, and Gregory Alexander. *Unholy Babylon: The Secret History of Saddam's War.* New York: St. Martin's Press, 1991.

Davidson, Elishua. *Islam, Israel, and the Last Days.* Eugene, OR: Harvest House, 1991.

de Marenches, Count, and Christine Ockrent. *The Evil Empire: The Third World War Now.* London: Sidgwick and Jackson, 1988.

———, and David A. Andelman. *The Fourth World War: Diplomacy and Espionage in the Age of Terrorism.* New York: William Morrow and Company, 1992.

Dershowitz, Alan. *The Case for Israel.* Hoboken, NJ: John Wiley and Sons, 2003.

Dunnigan, James F. *How to Make War: A Comprehensive Guide to Modern Warfare.* New York: William Morrow, 1982.

Editors of the *Talmud* and *Midrash* and *Rabbinical Sources. Daniel.* Brooklyn: Mesorah Publications, 1980.

———. *Genesis.* Translated by Rabbi Meir Zlotowitz. Brooklyn: Mesorah Publications, 1980.

———. *Yechezkel: The Book of Ezekiel.* Brooklyn: Mesorah Publications, 1980.

Ellisen, Stanley A. *Who Owns the Land? The Arab Israeli Conflict.* Portland, OR: Multnomah, 1991.

Esposito, John L., ed. *The Oxford History of Islam.* Oxford: Oxford University Press, 1999.

Gabriel, Mark A. *Islam and the Jews.* Lake Mary, FL: Charisma House, 1984.

Gilbert, Martin. *The Routledge Atlas of the Arab-Israeli Conflict.* 8th ed. Abingdon, England: Routledge, 2005.

Glubb, John. *A Short History of the Arab Peoples.* London: Hodder and Stoughton, 1969.

Hatina, Meir. *Islam and Salvation in Palestine: The Islamic Jihad Movement.* Tel Aviv: Tel Aviv University, 2001.

Hennecke, Edgar. *New Testament Apocrypha.* Translated by R. McLachan, Wilson. Philadelphia: Westminster, 1965.

Herman, Edward S., and Gerry O'Sullivan. *The "Terrorism" Industry: The Experts and Institutions That Shape Our View of Terror.* New York: Pantheon Books, 1989.

Hersh, Seymour M. *The Samson Option.* New York: Random House, 1991.

Hertz, J. H., ed. *The Pentateuch and Haftorahs.* London: Soncino Press, 1961.

Hindson, Ed. *Approaching Armageddon.* Eugene, OR: Harvest House, 1997.

Huntington, Samuel P. *The Clash of Civilizations and the Remaking of World Order.* New York: Simon and Schuster, 1996.

Jeffrey, Grant R. *War on Terror: Unfolding Bible Prophecy.* Toronto: Frontier Research Publications, 2002.

Josephus, Flavius. *Josephus.* Translated by William Whiston. Grand Rapids: Kregel Publications, 1960.

Kepel, Gilles. *Jihad: The Trail of Political Islam.* Translated by Anthony F. Roberts. Cambridge, MA: Belknap Press of Harvard University Press, 2002.

Kremers, Marion F. *God Intervenes in the Middle East.* Shippensburg, PA: Companion Press, 1992.

Lewis, David Allen, and Jim Fletcher. *The Last War: The Failure of the Peace Process and the Coming Battle for Jerusalem.* Green Forest, AR: New Leaf Press, 2001.

Lindsay, Hal. *The Final Battle.* Palos Verdes, CA: Western Front, 1995.

Livingston, Robert. *Christianity and Islam: The Final Clash; a Look at the Church, Radical Islam, Israel, and America in End-Time Bible Prophecy.* Enumclaw, WA: Pleasant Word, 2004.

Livingstone, Neil C. *The Cult of Counterterrorism: The Weird World of Spooks, Counterterrorists, Adventurers, and Not Quite Professionals.* Lexington, MA: Lexington Books, 1990.

Mauro, Ryan. *Death to America: The Unreported Battle of Iraq.* Baltimore: PublishAmerica, 2005.

Miller, Judith, and Laurie Mylroie. *Saddam Hussein and the Crisis in the Gulf.* New York: Times Books, 1990.

Mohammed. *The Koran.* Translated by George Sale. Philadelphia: J. W. Moore, 1850.

———. *The Meaning of the Glorious Koran.* Translated by Marmaduke Pickthall. New York: Dorset Press, (n.d.).

Mordecai, Victor. *Is Fanatic Islam a Global Threat?* Springfield, MO: Talmidim, 1996.

Mylroie, Laurie. *Study of Revenge: Saddam Hussein's Unfinished War Against America.* Washington DC: AEI Press, 2000.

Pentecost, Dwight J. *Things to Come: A Study in Biblical Eschatology.* Grand Rapids: Dunham, 1958.

Peters, George. *The Theocratic Kingdom.* Grand Rapids: Kregel, 1957.

Peters, Joan. *From Time Immemorial: The Origins of the Arab-Israeli Conflict over Palestine.* New York: Harper and Row, 1984.

Price, Randall. *In Search of Temple Treasures: The Lost Ark and the Last Days.* Eugene, OR: Harvest House, 1994.

———. *Jerusalem in Prophecy.* Eugene, OR: Harvest House, 1998.

Ragg, Lonsdale, and Laura Ragg, eds. *The Gospel of Barnabas.* Rome: II Edizione, 1986.

Rosenau, Helen. *Vision of the Temple: The Image of the Temple in Jerusalem in Judaism and Christianity.* London: Oresko Books, 1979.

Saleem, Musa. *The Muslims and the New World Order.* London: ISDS Books, 1993.

Schmitt, John W., and J. Carl Laney. *Messiah's Coming Temple: Ezekiel's Prophetic Vision of the Future Temple.* Grand Rapids: Kregel, 1997.

Schwartau, Winn. *Information Warfare: Chaos on the Electronic Superhighway.* New York: Thunder's Mouth Press, 1994.

Smith, Wilbur M. *Israeli/Arab Conflict...and the Bible.* Glendale, CA: Regal Books, 1967.

Spencer, Robert. *The Politically Incorrect Guide to Islam and the Crusades.* Washington DC: Regnery Publishing, 2005.

Stein, Leonard. *The Balfour Declaration.* London: Vallentine, Mitchell, 1961.

Stobart, J. W. H. *Islam and Its Founder.* New York: E. and J. B. Young and Co., 1884.

Toffler, Alvin, and Heidi Toffler. *War and Anti-War: Survival at the Dawn of the 21st Century.* Boston: Little, Brown and Company, 1993.

Walvoord, John F. *The Nations in Prophecy.* Grand Rapids: Zondervan, 1976.

Wheatcroft, Andrew. *The Ottomans.* London: Viking, 1993.

Williams, Paul L. *The Al Qaeda Connection: International Terrorism, Organized Crime, and the Coming Apocalypse.* Amherst, NY: Prometheus Books, 2005.

# About the Author

GRANT R. JEFFREY is the author of twenty-three books, including *Armageddon, Prince of Darkness, Final Warning, Signature of God,* and *Finding Financial Freedom.* His decades of research on military history, intelligence, and prophecy are reflected in this latest book, *The Next World War.* Jeffrey's dozens of research trips to the Middle East and his extensive interviews with experts in the military and intelligence fields provide the background for the insights found in this book.

His books have been translated into twenty-four languages and have sold more than seven million copies throughout the world. His television program, *Bible Prophecy Revealed,* is broadcast weekly on Trinity Broadcasting Network. He also appears frequently as a guest on television and radio.

Jeffrey's passion for research has led him to acquire a personal library of more than seven thousand books on prophecy, theology, and biblical archaeology. He earned his master's degree and a doctor of philosophy in biblical studies from Louisiana Baptist University. Before becoming a full-time writer, he was a professional financial planner for eighteen years with his own brokerage company in western Canada.

# Also available from Grant R. Jeffrey

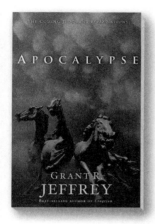

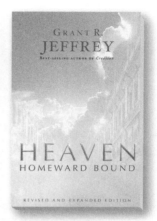

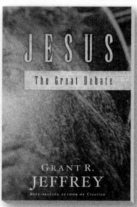

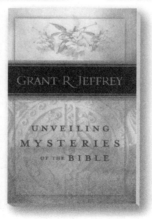

WATERBROOK PRESS

www.waterbrookpress.com

To learn more about WaterBrook Press and view
our catalog of products, log on to our Web site:
**www.waterbrookpress.com**

WATERBROOK
PRESS